REVOLUTION
FOR
GOLDEN KINGDOM

BEGAMPURA

(A Welfare State)

TO EXECUTE THE THOUGHT OF SATGURU RAVIDASS MAHARAJ JI
THE POLITICAL CONCEPT WILL BE FULFILLED

BY THREE-WAYS

By recognizing the Religion
By Capturing the Political Power
By becoming the Ruler

Sat Paul Virdi

CHRISTIANITY ISLAM JUDAISM SHINTO

HINDUISM BUDDISM RAVIDASSIA SIKHISM

Musalman So Dosti Hinduaun So Kar Preet|
Ravidas Jyoti Sab Ram Ki Sab Hai Apne Meet||(147)
"Satguru Ravidass Ji"

Means:

Oh. man! You should make friendship with Muslims and love Hindus, Because God's flame, in the shape of a Soul, i absorbed in every person. Therefore, all men are equal and friends.

Message

A sincere effort has been made to write this book `Revolution for Golden Kingdom **"Begampura"**, as per my concept and thinking and from the **angle** I am looking at the life and Bani of Satguru Ravidass Ji, it has motivated me to write this book. Through this book, I want to motivate the people who have suffered slavery for centuries under the inhuman Caste System of the Brahmanical order. And even today the oppressed society cannot enjoy its freedom. At some places they are beaten for riding a mare and at other places, they are killed for having a moustache. It makes me sad to see these inhumane systems and the suffering and condition of people living below the poverty line, hence, I have collected resourceful and historical information from various sources from history books, like a honey bee who works made for its hive. So, that common people can get information.

Doing an intensive analysis, readers should think about how to eliminate the Caste System, which is shameful for the modern Society of India, and I do hope that all readers, especially the young generation would get the knowledge and idea of the **Begampura** which Satguru Ravidass Ji gave, the unique concept for the benefit of citizens of the entire universe and made their human lives truly fruitful, to live happily without facing the conflicting nationalities, races, castes, and different religions, and take benefit from this book for the upliftment of the downtrodden to get the power i.e. Social, (Social justice, Social & cultural unity, spiritual unity and equality), Economic and political (Political power is the master key of all locks), that **how to capture the power and become the Ruler** of the Country.

This piece of sacred information will spark and play an essential role in the life of those who wish to bring equality, justice and prosperity into society and end the prevailing discrimination.

It is my humble advice to my brothers to write something and share with the community about their life experiences or choose any subject matter they know. Lots of people below the poverty line are looking for help, and your writing will be a medium of communication with the world, and some policies can be helped for the welfare of their help. Lastly, I thank to my friends for encouraging me in this noble work.

So Kat Jane Peer Prai|
Ja Kai Antar Dard Na Pai||(40)

Satguru Ravidass Ji said in his hymn that: ``who has not suffered the pang of sufferings, himself, cannot understand the woes of others``

Sat Paul Virdi
BA LLB

Contents

Part – 1

By recognizing the religion

Part – 2

By capturing the political power

Part – 3

By becoming the ruler

Part- 1

Chapter - 1

By recognizing the religion

Know about the religion which has been given by the Satguru Ravidass Ji in the 14th century at the time of the Muslim empire and the slavery under Brahmanical Verna System, During that period though Brahmin was not in power even then they behaved with Shudras like animals. Now this is the time to change the concept of the *Manu-wadi* Brahmanical system in which they consider themselves as superhuman beings and upper class with love and brotherhood as per the teaching of Satguru Ravidass Ji.

Satguru Ravidass Ji

In the fourteenth century, India passed through a period of political turmoil and social decadence. In this world torn by hate and religious strife, a divinely-ordained event took place. In 1377 AD (1433 Vikarmi-Sambat), Shri Santokh Dass Ji and Mata Kalsi Devi Ji were blessed with a child (Satguru), Ravidass Ji, who was destined to be a teacher with an abiding message. From the very outset Satguru Ravidass Ji, the harbinger of Divine glory, displayed the holy spark in all his doings. He was a versatile personality and a charisma that no one could resist.Satguru Ravidass Ji, was a Divine and Godly Soul, preacher, reformer, and revolutionary religious leader. He proudly identified himself with the so-called lower caste (Chamar/Cobbler). Satguru Ravidass Ji always stood for the oppressed and downtrodden people. For him, social status, asceticism or power had no meaning or charm. While he met the obligations towards his own family, he always wanted and worked for the betterment of the whole of humanity. He enriched people with moral and religious values. He emphasized the unity of all religions and the futility of ceremonial and ritualistic worship.

He is recognised across the globe and in different cultures by the name of "Satguru Ravidass Ji". He was also worshipped as a Satguru by the Kings and Queens of that era. The world today needs to know about Satguru Ravidass Ji, the Prophet of the Ravidassia Religion who preached the gospel of universal brotherhood, love, fraternity, equality and casteless society. In the world of conflicting nationalities, races, castes and different religions, Satguru Ravidass Ji's gospel is that there is only one God. God is the Father/creator of all. This is the Satguru mantra (technic/Idea) for Begampura, peace and prosperity. He had lived a struggle and meaningful life during the Bhakti movement and condemned the unjust Brahmanical system, preached against casteism and in favour of humanity.

In 1528 AD Guru Ji at the age of 151 years left for his heavenly abode. The concept of Universal brotherhood, Justice, equality, tolerance, and Social, Economic and religious freedom for everybody has been preached by Satguru Ravidass Ji in the Shabad of **Begampura.**

*****

8

Chapter - 2

Religion

The meaning and definition of Religion

Religion is a complex and multifaceted concept that can be defined in various ways, depending on cultural, historical, and philosophical perspectives. Generally speaking, religion is a set of beliefs, practices, and values that are focused on the worship of a deity or deities, or on the pursuit of a particular moral or spiritual code.

Religion can involve the use of prayer, meditation, and ritual, as well as adherence to certain customs and traditions. It may also involve a belief in an afterlife or in reincarnation, and a concern for ethical principles such as justice, compassion, and forgiveness. The term religion is often used to describe a specific system of beliefs and practices, such as Christianity, Islam, Judaism, Buddhism, or Hinduism. However, religion can also refer to more general concepts, such as spirituality, faith, or belief in a higher power or purpose.

It is important to note that religion can have both positive and negative effects, depending on how it is practised and interpreted. While religion can offer a sense of community, meaning, and comfort for many people, it can also lead to conflict, discrimination, and intolerance when used to justify extremist or intolerant beliefs and actions.

In another view, the German Great thinker Karl Marx says that "Religion is the Opium of the people". (Devon Hyde says that Religion has actually convinced people that there is an invisible man living in the sky, who watches everything you do every day, and the invisible man has a special list of 10 things. He does not want you to do. If you do any of these 10 things, he has a special place full of fire, smoke, burning, torture and anguish. Where he will send you to live and suffer, and burn, and choke, and scream, and cry forever, and ever till the end of time. But he loves you! He loves it, and he needs money. He always need money. He is

9

all-powerful, all-perfect, all-knowing, it all-wise, and somehow, Just cannot handle money).

In other words, religion is the source of power with the followers and a way of life where the priest holds the command (sway) over the followers. Worship, moral conduct and there are so many other meanings of the religion as per their faith and beliefs.

In the world, there are so many religions, faith and beliefs. it is estimated that there are thousands of different religions and belief systems in the world, ranging from the major world religions like Christianity, Islam, Buddhism, Hinduism, Ravidassia, and Sikhism, to smaller, indigenous or local religions, and newer religious movements and spiritual practices.

(The sign and symbols of the main religions)

The definition of religion is a specific system of religious belief in a God or Gods and the associated practises, as well as the relationship of people to things they view as holy, sacred, absolute, spiritual, divine, or deserving of special reverence. The Hindu religion is no religion but a cultural living system in India called Hinduism. Hinduism believes in

10

many Gods and rebirth based on the Karama theory and Brahmanical System, which believe in Varna System, i.e. 1. Brahmin 2. Kastrya 3. Vaish 4. Sudras also believes in Casteism and discrimination, even not Humanitarian. The fourth Varana is called Sudras, who are the original Native of India, i.e. Bharat. That's why so many saints, prophets, Satguru and Social reformers condemned the Varna System of Brahminical and wanted to reform it, but still, there are so many evil things in Hinduism.

So, many communities left Hinduism and formed other religions like Buddhism, Jainism, and Sikhism. Shudras and Ashoots are still non-confirmative Hindus and are changing their religion to another religion, this one or that one, but they feel not own house, because of inequality, discrimination, and casteism. So many people have adopted the Muslim, Christian, Sikh and Buddhist religions.

In Punjab, the majority adopted Sikhism and believed that Sikhism was the best religion formed by Guru Nanak Dev Ji. The Sikh Gurus in which, the holy Bani of Saints and Satguru Ravidass ji and Satguru Kabir ji, has also been included by Guru Arjan Dev Ji in the year 1604 AD. But like Hinduism, the same things happened in Sikhism also. Some lobbies comprising a few persons became fascist and communal, practised discrimination against lower castes, and believe in casteism against the philosophy of Gurus. Ravidassia people felt discriminated against and depressed and decided to form a new religion, i.e. **"Ravidassia"**. **Ravidassia community is known mainly Chamar, Jatav, Ahirwar, Kureel, Dhusia, Ramdasia, Ravidassia, and Satnami are 22,496,047 54 as per the list which has prepared in the year1950, which is now outdated,** moreover, the list of Scheduled castes in India, the Indian constitution, in *Constitution (Scheduled Castes) Order, 1950* lists 1,109 castes across 28 states in its First Schedule, while the *Constitution (Scheduled Tribes) Order, 1950* lists 744 tribes across 22 states in its First Schedule. **Ravidassia** are called by about 40 different names in different places and in the state of India, as mentioned below in the list:-

1	Ad Dharmi (Pb.& oth.St.)	2	Asadaru (G) (Knt)
3	Asodi (G) Knt M	4	Bairwa (MP)
5	Balahi (Hry)	6	Batoi (H)
7	Bhambhi (G) H	8	Chamadia(G)
9	**Chamar (Pb)**	10	Chamar Rehgar (Pb)
11	Chamgar (G)	12	Charamkaar (Bihar)
13	Dhusia (Uknd)	14	Harali (G) Knt
15	Jatav / Jatava (UP)	16	Jatia (Pb,H & HP)
17	Jhusia (Uknd)	18	Kamti (G)
19	Khalpa (G)	20	Machigar (G)
21	Madar (Gujrat)Knt	22	Madig (Gujrat)
23	Madiga (AP) &Telgana	24	Mochi (Raj)
25	Nalia (G)	26	Nona (Maharastra)
27	Ramdasia **(Pb)**	28	Ramdasia Sikh **(Pb)**
29	Ranigar (G)	30	Ravidasia Sikh **(Pb)**
31	**Ravidassia (Pb)**	32	Rehgar (HP)
33	Rishi (Assam)	34	Rohidas (Bihar)
35	Rohit (Gujrat)	36	Samagar(AP),Telangana
37	Samgar (R)& (G) Knt	38	Satnami (MP)
39	Surjyabanshi (M)		

All these are the Charamkar (cobblers), who are doing the work of tanning the skin/leather and making shoes, garments and other goods from the skin of the dead animal. All the persons, as mentioned earlier, believe in the Ravidassia religion and consider Satguru Ravidass Ji as their Guru.

*****

Chapter - 3

Ravidassia Religion

In a world of conflicting nationalities, they have racism, casteism, and different religions. Love and Fraternity become meaningless if there is a hindrance of Religion and Casteism among humanity. Casteism is a hateful principle of Brahmanical. In the 15th century, Satguru Ravidass Ji's preached that one God is the Father of all and is the Guru mantra for love, peace and prosperity. The concept of Universal brotherhood, equality for all, Justice, i.e. Social, Political and Economical for all, tolerance and religious freedom to everybody, Morality, and Ethics has given the new concept of a welfare State, i.e. Begampura, to save humanity. Satguru Ravidass ji has written a Granth consisting of the Shabads and Saloks, i.e. called, Amritbani. It is a new religious Holy Granth (scripture), i.e. called Amritbani of Satguru Ravidass Ji. Satguru Ravidass ji said that:

Ravidass Jeh Granth Hai, Parrai Sunai Mann Laye |
Sab Hi Pdarath Milegai, Eisse Sabh Bar Paaye ||

Means:- Ravidass Ji says to his devotees to read the holy scripture and listen to it whole heartedly, and then you will get all riches and boons from this Granth.

Satguru Ravidass Ji travelled to many states of India and middle Asia. Satguru Ravidass ji, Gave the massage of Begumpura to the whole world's people. Large numbers of people and Kings and Queens became followers of Satguru Ravidass Ji. Guru Nanak Dev Ji fetched the holy Bani of Satguru Ravidass Ji, and from this Bani 40 Shabad and one Saloke has written in the sacred Guru Granth Sahab Ji by 5th Guru Arjan Dev Ji. That was why the Ravidassia community has faith in the holy Guru Granth Sahab Ji, and mostly in Punjab aria adopted Sikhism by them and known as Ravidassi Sikh.

After Satguru Ravidass Ji, the teaching and philosophy of Satguru Ravidass Ji were spread in the world by many Saints and by followers. So many poets and singers sing the Holi Shabad, writers have

13

written many books about Satguru and thinkers, and preachers have also preached and said about Satguru Ravidass ji. The Bani of Satguru Ravidass ji has travelled and taken a new name, i.e., Holi Granth Amritbani. Thousand of Dera of Ravidassia exist in India. The main Dera who are spreading the teaching and philosophy of Satguru Ravidass ji`s are "Dera 108 Sant Sarwan Dass, Sachkhand Ballan, Jalandhar, Swami Jagat Giri Ashram Pathankot Punjab, Dera Sachkhand Pandwa, Phagwara, Dera Khuralgarh Sahib Garhshanker, Hoshiarpur, Dera Sant Baba Phool Nath Ji Chaheru Phagwara, Dera 108 Sant Baba Mela Ram Ji, Bharo Mazara Nawanshahr, Dera Sant Shri Tehal Das Maharaj ji. Salem Tabri Ludhiana, Dera baba lal das ji kapal Mochan Yamunanagar Haryana, and many other Deras in the Punjab and Haryana as well as in the India.

But the scenario was changed when Shri 108 Sant Niranjan Dass Ji Head of the Dera 108 Sant Sarwan Dass, Sachkhand Ballan, Jalandhar, along with 108 Sant Rama Nand Ji were on a Europe tour on a mission to preach and spread the teaching of Shri Guru Ravidass Ji. When both saints with the followers reached Austria`s capital Viana Shri Guru Ravidass Mandir on 24th May 2009, When the Sikh extremists attacked Sant Niranjan Dass Ji and Ramanand Ji while sitting inside of Shri Guru Ravidass Mandir in Vienna, Austria, Sant Ramanand Ji left for heaven on 24th May 2009 morning and Sant Niranjan Dass Ji was hit by two bullets and received serious injuries and admitted in the hospital, then came back to India.

This all happened with pre-planning and our Ravidassia community was deeply hurt and reacted aggressively and decided to declare separate independent Ravidassia religion, after that on 30th January 2010 at Janam Asthan Mandir, Seer Goverdhan, Varanasi, U.P. Where lakhs of devotees from India and abroad were present this day and in the presence of Sant Samaj, a Historic decision to form a separate Ravidassia Religion was taken unanimously. This decision was welcomed by one and all. The large numbers of people and their Saints from Chamar, Balmiki, and Kabirpanthi communities gathered and adopted the new Religion immediately.

On 30.01.2010, the Ravidassia Religion has been revived and declared that in the future all who consider Satguru Ravidass Ji as their Guru and have separate faith and they will be called Ravidassia. The efforts are to make the community educated, wise, strong, and organized to face every life challenge and solve it, to find out the solution to the challenge that nobody should be the victim of discrimination in the hand of Upper Castes.

The Present Guru (Priest) of Ravidassia Religion Sant Niranjan Dass Ji

Sant Niranjan Dass Ji was born on 6th January 1942 at village Ramdass Pur near Allawalpur in District Jalandhar to father Shri Sadhu Ram Ji and mother, Shrimati Rukmani Ji. Sant Niranjan Dass remained at the Dera and started doing Sewa at the Dera-Sant Sarwan Dass Ji named him "Hawaigar" ("speedy one"). He grew up serving at the feet of Sant Sarwan Dass Ji and later with Sant Hari Dass Ji and Sant Garib Dass Ji. After Sant Garib Dass Ji left for his heavenly abode on 23rd July 1994, Sant Niranjan Dass Ji was installed as Gaddi-Nashin (spiritual leader) of

Dera Sachkhand Ballan on 9th August 1994. He started with developing all projects devoted to the service of humankind in earnest, and the Dera has made tremendous progress under his guidance.

A lot of construction work has been done and is going on for the public welfare at Dera Sant Sarwan Dass Sachkhand Ballan, Jalandhar Pb. as well as at Varanasi UP Shri Guru Ravidass Janam Asthan Mandir. A large number of followers have adopted the Ravidassia religion under the blessings of Sant Niranjan Dass Ji. The president of India Sh. K.R. Narayanan along with Shri Kanshi Ram President of the Bahujan Samaj Party has visited for the inauguration of the Construction of the Gate in the name of Satguru Ravidass ji at Vanaras near BHU and placed the Gold Dome on Shri Guru Ravidass Janam Asthan Mandir at Seer Goverdhan Varanashi UP. Sh. Kanshi Ram ji said on that occasion that the Golder Era of Dalit has been started. Chief Minister Kumari Mayawati has developed a beautiful Park and a Ghat was made at the Bank of Ganga River in the name of Satguru Ravidass Ji when she was Chief Minister of Uttar Pradesh.

The Prime Minister Sh. Narinder Modi, Chief Minister Sh. Aditia Natha Jogi Ji has also given Rs.50/- crores in the year 2019 for the development of the birthplace Mandir of Satguru Ravidass ji. Sh. Rahul Gandhi ji Congress president of India, Smt. Priyanka Gandhi, Chief Minister Arvind Kejriwal Ex-Chief Minister Sh. Akhilesh Yadav and many other dignities came for paying the obeisance at the birthplace of Shri Guru Ravidass Janam Asthan Mandir at Seer Goverdhan Varanashi UP and get the blessing from Sant Niranjan Dass JI after touching their feet.

September 2021 Chief Minister Sardar Parkash Singh Badal, Chief Minister Captain Amarinder Singh, and Deputy Chief Minister Sukhvir Singh Badal visited the Dera and obeisance At Dera 108 Sant Sarwan Dass Sachkhand Ballan, Jalandhar, Punjab.

Chief Minister Sardar Charanjit Singh Channi has given Rs.50/- Crors for the opening of Satguru Ravidass Bani Adhyan Center near Dera

Ballan Jalandhar Punjab under the chairmanship of Sant Niranjan Dass ji and now the present Chief Minister Sardar Bhagwant Singh Maan has also confirmed that the Satgur Ravidass Bani Adhyan Center will be open shortly, even the Government of Punjab have to expend Rs.500/- Crores for this project.

Sant Rama Nand Ji

www.sachkhandballan.net

Shri 108 Sant Rama Nand Ji was born on February 2, 1952, in the house of blessed parents Shri Mehnga Ram Ji and Shrimati Jeet Kaur Ji. He was saintly from very birth. Sant Ramanand was an enlightened, spiritual and social personality. Society highly respected and revered him, particularly the Dalits and other less privileged in Punjab and elsewhere in India and abroad.

While Shri 108 Sant Niranjan Dass Ji Maharaj presents spiritual head, Dera Sachkhand Ballan and Sant Rama Nand Ji was a minister of Guru-Ghar exponent of Gurbani kirtan, a devotee of God, great 'Vaidya',

17

While remembering Shahid Sant Ramanand Ji, his efforts to commemorate Guru Ravidass Maharaj's birthplace near the BHU campus, Seer Govardhan Pur, Varanasi, UP. We must remember his sacrifice was to strengthen the sovereignty of the community and the ideological thoughts of Guru Ravidass Ji in a dignified way. In the end, the reflection of whatever you carry remains here.

If the land of Doaba in Punjab is known as a stronghold of Ravidassia, then it's because of their hardcore support and sacrifice. If any atrocity happens to any individual, then the voices of resistance come from Doaba, Punjab, first. The whole movement of the Bahujan Samaj Party and affiliated sister organizations began in the land of Punjab. Saheb Kanshi Ram was from Punjab. If you admire the Bhim Army, only the most significant support comes from that area. Whatever Ravidassia ideas you have these days, they come from the reality of Punjabi society

<u>At Vanarasi Uttar Pardesh India</u>

30 Jan 2010, people in crores from all communities and Saints of different religion 's as well as from the many country of the world in a big gatherings adopted the Ravidassia religion and they have adopted the rule and regulation of ravidassia religion.

18

The definition of the Ravidassia Religion

"Ravidassia Religion preached and based on the Universal Truth, Gospel of Universal Brotherhood, Love and Fraternity, Equality, Humanity, and Casteless Society, based on Logical concepts supported by the public".

The majority accepted the Principles of the newly formed Religion. The concept of "Ravidassia" Religion is clear:

- The Amritbani of Satguru Ravidass ji, containing the Holy Hymns of Satguru Ravidass Ji, was declared as religious Holy Granth of the newly formed Ravidassia Religion- **"Amritbani".**

- The place of Pilgrimage is Shri Guru Ravidass **Janam Asthan Mandir** Seer Govardhan Varanasi, Uttar Pradesh, India.

- The Sign of the Ravidassia religion is **"Har"** (Religious Symbol)

- The salutation is **"Jai Gurdev"** – Dhan Gurdev.

The objectives: To follow the Bani and teachings of Satguru

Ravidass Ji, besides the teachings and thoughts of propaganda Maharishi Bhagwan Valmik Ji, Satguru Namdev Ji, Satguru Kabir Ji, Satguru Trilochan Ji, Satguru Sain Ji and Satguru Sadhna Ji would also be propagated. To respect all religions, love humanity and lead a virtuous life.

The Concept of the Ravidassia religion is clear. The prophet is Satguru Ravidass Ji, Religion is Ravidassia, Place of worship is the birthplace Mandir of Satguru Ravidass at Seer Govardhan pur, Vanaras, UP. The aim is to respect all religions, love humanity, lead a virtuous life and work for the betterment of society without discrimination, eliminate slavery, and uplift the downtrodden. The Followers of the Ravidassia Religion live in each part of India and in the world in Large numbers. They have their own Ravidassia Mandir, Gurudwaras, Dham, Guru Ghar and Ravidassia Dharamshala.

Now the Ravidassia are willing and seeking that the government of India should give Constitutional recognition to the "Ravidassia" as a separate independent religion. But the Brahmanical Governments are not following the Constitution as they are not giving Justice, and rights to the oppressed, even not providing education. Public needs Jobs and facilities as required as per their population. This Brahmanical system forced the oppressed community to become poor and remain illiterate and untouchable.

Madho Abidia Hit Keen|
Bibek Dip Maleen Rahaao||
(Satguru Ravidass Ji) **Shabad || 14 ||**

Means: That `O God! Man loves illiteracy and ignorance. The lamp of his knowledge has become dim. The thoughtless are born again as creeping things; they cannot distinguish between good and evil.

Sat Vidiyan Ko Parai Prapat Karai Sada Gian|
Ravidass Kahai Bin Vidiya Nar Ko Jan Ajan||
(Satguru Ravidass Ji) **Shabad ||230||**

This means: That Everybody should learn the proper education and acquire knowledge. Ravidass says without education, and the man is ignorant.

So, education is a basic need and the birthright of humanity. Education is a foundation of awareness and consciousness. Without education, man can not develop his mind and become mindless, and a senseless man cannot build his business and become moneyless, a mindless and moneyless man does hard work the whole time and has no time for his own family, so he becomes timeless and if a man has no mind, no money, no time then automatically he becomes a slave. So, first of all, they should educate themselves, their children, and Society but remember one thing immoral and unethical education can be dangerous for humanity, as Aryan used this method against Shudras.

Satsangat Mil Raheeai Madhaoo |
Jaise Madhup Makhira ||

(Satguru Ravidass Ji) **Shabad || 16 ||**

Means: O my followers, continue to associate with each other as the honey bee with the bee-hive?

Regarding ORGANISATION as the honey bee with the bee-hive. The public has to learn and spread the teaching of Satguru Ravidass Ji so that awareness would prevail and can organize among all people & communities in the world on one platform so that we can fulfil the message of Satguru Ravidass Ji, to achieve the goal of Begampura.

Efforts made for Recognizing the Religion

Efforts were made to unite and form an Organisation of a majority of the Ravidassia to stand under one umbrella.

On 22.03.2020 in India, due to Covid-19 (a disease, namely Corona), Prime Minister Narinder Modi announced for lockdown and a Curfew was imposed suddenly. Then these days public was confined in their houses and suffering, and the poor public also stun on this sudden decision taken by the Prime Minister and on his announcement. It was a sudden collapse for the Poor Public. Their children were hungry. They were searching for food, water, medicine and looking for shelter. All institutions, businesses and factories were closed. All Shops were closed. Even all Religious Places, Mandir, mosques, churches and Gurdwaras, were closed. A total curfew was imposed, and Police men were beatings the public who come out of the house for food and medicine. It was a very difficult time for the public. Migrant Labour felt insecure, with no help from any side. Their job/work had gone, Labourers were migrating for working place in the hot days to their villages, houses & their's families were travelling one place to other without any vehicle. No bus, no car, no Train etc. all were stopped & due to this many labourers, men, women and children died without food, water. State Govt. as well as Center Government closed their eyes and not provided any little bits of help.

All TV Channels Closed their eyes, ears & mouth. Even our Prime Minister did not speak a single word. Only one NDTV Channel and Social Media National Dustak etc. were relaying and showing the heart-touching pictures which resisted sleep after watching the terrible scene.

During this lockdown (Curfew), 108 Sant Niranjan Dass Ji decided for providing the Langer to the public immediately and Hospital was Offered to the Govt., for Corona patients and Rs. One lac Donation was given to SSP, Jalandhar for Prime Minister relief Funds. Cooked Langer (food and distal water) has been provided in large in the surrounded areas. The massage has been given by Social Media by the writer as mentioned below:-

URGENT MESSAGE

We are making every effort to get our Ravidassia Religion incorporated in the Constitution of India for the benefit of our community.

We have chalked out a plan and appeal to all the Ravidassia who are residing in India and abroad, to write letters/representation or send E-Mails in their individual capacity to the following dignities requesting them to incorporate Ravidassia Religion in the constitution before the next Census 2021, to the following dignities:-

1. *Prime Minister of India*
2. *President of India*
3. *Registrar General and Census Commissioner, India*

The representatives of Ravidassia Mandirs ' Ravidassia Guru Ghars, Societies and Sabhas are also requested to write similarly to the above-said dignities on their letter pads. They should also make the people of their areas aware of this programme through announcements on loudspeakers of Guru Ghar, Press notes to every newspaper and also send the above-said message to the electronic media i.e. NDTV, News 24, Ajj Tak, etc. on their emails as well as this memorandum was also given to your area MLA, Member of Parliament (M.P), Ministers, Chief Ministers even the DC SDM by representation.

Let's commence this exercise on 15th-July-2020 and complete it till 30th-September, 2020.

We not only hope but are sure that we will succeed in our united effort.

With kind Regards
(General Secretary)

The memorandum was written on 15.07.2020 by the writer as mentioned below:-

Memorandum

1. We, crores of Ravidassia and Indian Citizens, belonging to the Scheduled Castes of Ad-Dharmi, Chamar, Mochi, Jatav, Rehgar, Charam Kaar etc., are proud followers of Sant Shiromani Satguru Ravidass Ji. Satguru Ravidass Ji was born in Varanasi, U.P. in 1377 AD and brought a heavenly message of humanity, brotherhood, peace, equality and prosperity of all. Satguru Ji's divinely message and blessing to society in the form of Gurbani is worshipped as Amritbani in many Satguru

23

Ravidass Temples and Gurudwara's.

2. All the followers of Satguru Ravidass Ji are called Ravidassia as they follow the Ravidassia Religion. In the last population census of 2011, lakhs of Ravidassia had to write Ravidassia in the "Other" column. Therefore, We humbly request your good self to include a religious column and allocate a unique code for Ravidassia Religion in the upcoming population census of 2021 and in all future population censuses so that the Ravidassia may be counted separately.

3. This will be a revolutionary step by your good self and will give crores of Ravidassia their own identity. By taking this revolutionary step, your good self will be doing justice to crores of followers of Sant Shiromani Satguru Ravidass Ji and for this, they will always be thankful to you.

(Gen. Secretary)

In the number Lacs of Regtd. Letters, and Massage through what's app and by E-mail were sent to the Hon`ble  Prime Minister of India, the Hon`ble President of India, and the Commission/Director of Census Board. It becomes a massive movement by the Ravidassia community. We made banners to create a new column in the census form 2021 as   RAVIDASSIA. Every Village has arranged a meeting for awareness among the public.

The Census work on March 21st 2021, also started in the United Kingdom (UK). UK has allotted us the Ravidassia Column and our organizations and one of the British Ravidassia Council UK. We are very keen to see and did a good job organising and educating our people to write in the column of religion as Ravidassia as well as Ravidassia in the ethnic group. In the UK Census result, ten thousand people were initially reported as Ravidassia.

Religion Movement

Power comes from religion, such as organizing and generating power. If Ravidassia successfully organises the people on one platform all over India, then the Ravidassia Religion can successfully educate the people resulting in a big organization. To agitate or execute the power to get the rights, Ravidassia can successfully achieve the concept of Begampura. So, Ravidassia will be a big organization as a new separate and independent Religion known as "Ravidassia".

Jo Bole, So, Nirbhay |
Satguru Ravidass Maharaj Ji Ki, Jay ||

Means:- who will say Satguru Ravidass Maharaj Ji Ki Jay, those who speak are fearless. How and why they will be fearless because Satguru Ravidass Maharaj Ji, divine power and Crores of peoples, are standing with you. Then nobody will dared to touch you or commit the lynching with the follower of Satguru Ravidass Ji Maharaj. That's why we are saying "Jai Gur Dev ".

To boost the followers' moral to be fearless and motivate them to overcome fear and eliminate slavery and poverty.

The question is, what should Ravidassia do for the betterment and welfare of the community in future? Is there any road map or future plan after giving them an independent Ravidassia Religion?

Satguru Ravidass Ji has given the concept of Begampura, which clearly describes the idea of the welfare state. We should understand the meaning of Holi Hymn (Shabad) of Begampura, which is also written in the Holi Granth of Sikhs, "Guru Granth Sahib."

*****

Chapter - 4

Concept of Begampura

"Begampura", the Holy hymn (Shabad), was narrated by Satguru Ravidass Ji in the 15th Century. This Shabad has also written in the Shri Guru Granth Sahib, which was compiled in the year 1604-AD by Shri. Guru Arjan Dev Ji, the fifth Guru laid the foundations of a system of society following the principle that everyone should have equal rights (egalitarian) in the world of order blessed with peace and happiness for all. The Begampura means a welfare state, as Satguru Ravidass Ji has preached in the **Shabad**

Begampura

ਬੇਗਮਪੁਰਾ ਸਹਰ ਕੋ ਨਾਉ ॥

ਦੂਖੁ ਅੰਦੋਹੁ ਨਹੀ ਤਿਹਿ ਠਾਉ ॥

ਨਾਂ ਤਸਵੀਸ ਖਿਰਾਜੁ ਨ ਮਾਲੁ ॥

ਖਉਫੁ ਨ ਖਤਾ ਨ ਤਰਸੁ ਜਵਾਲੁ ॥੧॥

ਅਬ ਮੋਹਿ ਖੂਬ ਵਤਨ ਗਹ ਪਾਈ ॥

ਊਹਾਂ ਖੈਰਿ ਸਦਾ ਮੇਰੇ ਭਾਈ ॥੧॥ਰਹਾਉ॥

ਕਾਇਮੁ ਦਾਇਮੁ ਸਦਾ ਪਾਤਿਸਾਹੀ ॥

ਦੋਮ ਨ ਸੇਮ ਏਕ ਸੋ ਆਹੀ ॥

ਆਬਾਦਾਨੁ ਸਦਾ ਮਸਹੂਰ ॥

ਊਹਾਂ ਗਨੀ ਬਸਹਿ ਮਾਮੂਰ ॥੨॥

ਤਿਉ ਤਿਉ ਸੈਲ ਕਰਹਿ ਜਿਉ ਭਾਵੈ ॥

ਮਹਰਮ ਮਹਲ ਨ ਕੋ ਅਟਕਾਵੈ ॥

ਕਹਿ ਰਵਿਦਾਸ ਖਲਾਸ ਚਮਾਰਾ ॥

ਜੋ ਹਮ ਸਹਰੀ ਸੁ ਮੀਤੁ ਹਮਾਰਾ ॥੩॥੨॥

Satguru Ravidass ji said about Begampura

SHABAD || 3 ||

Begam Pura Sahar Ko Naao ||

Dukh Andohu Nahi Tihi Thaao ||

Nan Tasvis Khiraj Na Mal ||

Khauf Na Khata Na Taras Javal || 1 ||

Ab Mohi Khub Vatan Gah Paie ||

Uhan Khair Sada Mere Bhaie || 1 ||rahaao||

Kayam Dayam Sada Patisahi ||

Dom Na Sem Ek So Ahi ||

Abadan Sada Mashur ||

Uhan Gani Baseh Mamur || 2 ||

Teo Teo Sail Karahi Jeo Bhavai ||

Mahram Mahal Na Ko Atkavai ||

Kahi Ravidass Khalas Chamara ||

Jo Ham Sahri So Meet Hamara || 3 || 2 ||

This means : That there is a city named Begampura. There is no place for pain and sorrow. There is no fear of imposing taxes or of tribute (Kharaj). There is no care nor sin, nor dread nor death. Now I have found an excellent abode where ceaseless happiness reigns, and God's sovereignty is firm and ever existing. There is no second or third-rate citizen. Everybody is equal there. Inhabited and ever-famous is that city. Its citizens are fully dowered by wealth. They wander there as they, please. Nobody restrains them from going hither and thither. Ravidass, an emancipated tanner, says, O, my friend! Come and become my fellow citizens of Begampura.

Establishment of a world order like "Begampura". With unity, equality and brotherhood for all. Human beings would enjoy a universal brotherhood free of discrimination based on colour, caste, creed, dependence, slavery and worldly attachments. Every citizen of

"Begampura" will enjoy complete social, political, cultural and spiritual equality with full human rights. Satguru Ravidass Ji laid the foundations of an egalitarian, democratic republic for humanity.

Establishing such an institutional order in this world would lead to the resolution of all problems confronting the world.

Begampura Sahar Ko Naao|
Dukh Andohu Nahi Tihi Thaao||

Satguru Ravidass Ji Maharaj says he is a citizen of the world known as "Begampura", devoid of grief. There is no room for any pain and worry in that world. **OR** - The governance of this world should be based on the principles of "Begampura", in which all citizens are equal and where freedom, equality, justice and universal brotherhood prevail all the time. All human beings would have equal rights, and all citizens' basic needs would be fulfilled. Everyone will have equal human rights there. All living beings in "Begampura" would be free of grief. No one would ever suffer from any pain and suffering because of discrimination because of high or low caste, untouchability, affluence–poverty and colour like white or black etc.

Nan Tasvis Khiraj Na Mal |
Khauf Na Khata Na Taras Jawal ||1||

There is neither any worry nor tension in "Begampura" city. No one has to pay any taxes for trading in God's Naam. All citizens of that "Begampura" are free of any fear, discord, felony, desire, pity, and scarcity, and they are all one with God. **OR** - Every living being in the "Begampura" world is free of worry and tension. No one is forced to pay taxes.

One and all enjoy complete human rights and do their duty free of any fear of tyranny, tension, felony and deprivation.

Ab Mohi Khub Vatan Gah Paie|
Uhan Khair Sada Mere Bhai ||1||Rahaao ||

28

Dear brother! I have now attained an eternal and blessed place in 'Begampura". This place has permanent, lasting peace. Therefore, every living being enjoyed lifelong happiness and stability in the "Begampura" world order.

Kayam Dayam Sada Patisahi |
Dom Na Sem Ek So Ahi ||

There is an eternal kingdom of God in that world, "Begampura". No one is second or third in command there, but there is only one kingdom of eternal God, the Almighty. **OR**- In this world order of "Begampura", there should be such permanent governance that ensures freedom, equality, justice and equal citizenship status for all humans. No one should be a second-class or third-class citizen.

Abadan Sada Masahur |
Uhan Gani Baseh Mamur ||2||

God's "Begampura" is well-known and always populated with blessed, noble souls. Fully satisfied, holy, noble souls reside there, free of any longings and always engrossed in deep meditation of God. **OR** - "Begampura" should be the famous abode of learned people where they live happily together, and everyone's basic needs of human life are always fulfilled.

Teo Teo Sail Karahi Jeo Bhavai |
Mahram Mahal Na Ko Atkavai ||

Residents of "Begampura" stroll freely as per their will. Well-versed with the palaces of Begampura, the resident souls walk freely anywhere without any hindrances. **OR** - The citizens of "Begampura" enjoy full human rights and can move anywhere without restriction. They can stroll anywhere according to their wishes.

Kahi Ravidass Khalas Chamara |
Jo Ham Sahri So Meet Hamara ||3||2||

Satguru Ravidass Ji Maharaj explains, "I have got rid of all worldly attachments through deep meditation of God. Any living being that gets free of such bonds is indeed pious. He is my friend and my fellow citizen." **OR** - Satguru Ravidass Ji says that all human citizens of "Begampura" should be free of discrimination because of caste, untouchability, slavery and attachment etc., and all citizens should ever live happily together in that world order.

This hymn (Shabad) is spiritual and religious, Maybe, but in my view, I have taken the idea from this Holy hymn (Shabad) as a political concept in which Satguru Ravidass Ji saying about the State, which should be like the thought of Satguru Ji as described in the Hymn/Shabad.

This message and concept regarding Socialism - Liberty, Equality, Fraternity, and Justice, i.e. Social, Religious, economic and political was given by Satguru Ravidass Ji in the 14th Century. After that, German philosopher Karl Marks has also given the theory of Socialism. **Karl Marks** gave the concept of Socialism in the 19th Century.

Karl Marks
(May 5, 1818–March 14, 1883)

Generations of political figures and socioeconomic thinkers have been affected by a Persian political economist who also worked as a writer, activist, and author of important writings, including **"The Communist Manifesto" and "Das Kapital."**

The leading theory of Karl Marx is the "Key Takeaways". A social, political, and economic doctrine known as Marxism emphasises the conflict between the working class and capitalists. Marx wrote that the power relationships between capitalists and workers were inherently exploitative and would inevitably create class conflict.

The definition of Marxism is the theory of Karl Marx, which says that society's classes are the cause of struggle and that a community should have no classes. An example of Marxism is **replacing private ownership with cooperative ownership**.

In short," take from the rich and give to the poor".

According to Karl Marx's views, most rich people became rich by depriving the poor people of honest wages and their due rights in jobs in the political system and economic world. Therefore, social, Political and Economic Equality are needed in Society.

In the Marxism theories, there are conflicts and struggles between the societies, but the teaching and philosophy of Satguru Ravidass Ji is the basis of love, fraternity, and non-violence. Therefore, there is no place for conflict or violence.

Musalman So Dosti Hinduaun So Kar Preet|
Ravidas Jyoti Sab Ram Ki Sab Hai Apne Meet||
(Satguru Ravidass Ji"(147)

Means: O man! You should make friends with Muslims and love Hindus because the flame of God, in the shape of the soul, is absorbed in every person. Therefore, all men are equal and friends

After that, in the 20th Century, Dr. B.R. Ambedkar raised the voice of the poor/ Shudras.

Bhimrao Ramji Ambedkar
(14 April 1891 – 6 December 1956)

Baba Sahab Dr B.R. Ambedkar was an Indian jurist, economist, social reformer and political leader who headed the drafting committee of the Constitution of India. He also served as Law and Justice minister in the first cabinet of Pt. Jawaharlal Nehru, and inspired the Dalit Buddhist movement after renouncing Hinduism.

Ambedkar graduated from Elphinstone College, University of Bombay, and studied economics at Columbia University and the London School of Economics, receiving doctorates in 1927 and 1923, respectively, and was among a handful of Indian students to have done so at either institution in the 1920s. He also trained in the law at Gray's Inn, London.

He was an economist, professor, and lawyer in his early career. His political activities marked his later life; he became involved in campaigning and negotiations for India's independence, publishing journals, advocating political rights and social freedom for Dalits, and contributing significantly to establishing the state of India. In 1956, he converted to Buddhism, initiating mass conversions of Dalits.

For the defence of Dalit rights, he started many periodicals like *Mook Nayak, Bahishkrit Bharat,* and *Equality Janta.*

He was appointed to the Bombay Presidency Committee to work with the all-European Simon Commisson in 1925. This commission sparked significant protests across India, and while most Indians ignored its report, Ambedkar wrote a separate set of recommendations for the future Constitution of India.

By 1927, Ambedkar had decided to launch active movements against untouchability. He began with public campaigns and marches to open up public drinking water resources that were out of Dalits' reach. He led a satyagraha in Mahad to fight for the right of the untouchable community to draw water from the main water tank of the town. In a conference in late 1927, Ambedkar publicly condemned the classic Hindu text, the Manusmriti (Laws of Manu), for ideologically justifying caste discrimination and "untouchability". He ceremonially burned copies of the ancient text. On 25 December 1927, he led thousands of followers to burn copies of Manusmriti. Thus annually, 25 December is celebrated as Manusmriti Dahan Din (Manusmriti Burning Day) by Ambedkarites and Dalits.

In 1930, Ambedkar launched the Kalaram Temple movement after three months of preparation. About 15,000 volunteers assembled at Kalaram Temple satyagraha, making one of the most extraordinary processions of Nashik. The procession was headed by a military band and a batch of scouts; women and men walked with discipline, order and determination to see the deity/god for the first time. When they reached the gates, the gates were closed by Brahmin authorities.

Poona Pact

In 1932, the British colonial government announced the formation of a separate electorate for "Depressed Classes" in the Communal Award. Mahatma Gandhi fiercely opposed a separate

33

electorate for untouchables, saying he feared that such an arrangement would divide the Hindu community. Gandhi protested by fasting while imprisoned in the Yerwada Central Jail of Poona.

As a result an agreement, known as the Poona Pact was signed between Ambedkar (on behalf of the depressed classes among Hindus) and Madan Mohan Malaviya (on behalf of the other Hindus). The agreement gave reserved seats for the depressed classes in the Provisional legislatures within the general electorate. Due to the pact, the depressed class received **148** seats in the legislature instead of 71, as allocated in the Communal Award proposed earlier by the colonial government under Prime Minister Ramsay MacDonald. The text used the term "Depressed Classes" to denote Untouchables among Hindus who were later called Scheduled Castes and Scheduled Tribes under the India Act of 1935 and later the Indian Constitution of 1950. In the Poona Pact, a unified electorate was formed in principle, but primary and secondary elections allowed the Untouchables in practice to choose their own candidates.

In 1990, the Bharat Ratna, India's highest civilian award, was posthumously conferred on Ambedkar. The salutation Jai Bhim (lit. "Hail Bhim") used by followers honours him. He is also referred to by the honorific **Babasaheb.**

And Babasaheb drafted the Indian constitution starting from the preamble:

" **We, THE PEOPLE OF INDIA**, having solemnly resolved to constitute India into a **SOVEREIGN, DEMOCRATIC, REPUBLIC** and to secure to all its citizens:

JUSTICE, social, economic and political;

LIBERTY of thought, expression, belief, faith and worship;

EQUALITY of status and opportunity; and to promote among them all

FRATERNITY assures the dignity of the individual and the unity and integrity of the Nation"

The concept of the Indian constitution is also based on non-violence and has no place for violence. It has given all citizens equal rights and social justice, but the century will be completed; governments failed to provide equality and justice to all citizens. Baba Sahab also presented his written lecture paper, ``THE ANNIHILATION OF CASTE,`` in the name of Satguru Ravidass Ji.

On December 6, 1956, Bawa Saheb took his last breath; Crors of Dalits felt as if their Godfather had gone and became a vacuum without a leader in the Dalit community.

Babu Jagjivan Ram Ji

Babu Jagjivan Ram was a Dalit leader, freedom fighter, a social reformer. He was in Congress Party and was a minister in the Government. In 1971, while he was the Defence Minister, Pakistan attacked India, and India won this war with Pakistan. The whole of India appreciated the work of Babu Jagjivan Ram ji. He left Congress in 1977 and joined the Janata Party alliance and his Congress for Democracy. All these parties agreed that the candidate for Prime Minister would be Babu Jagjivan Ram Ji. It is a historical moment, and the public thinks the coming elections will change the course of history and give a new lease of life to democracy and our democratic institutions and strengthen the power of the people.

The Dalit Community expected he would be our leader and become the PM of India. Instead, he tried to become the PM of India. Still, the Upper Caste leaders deceived him and made him Dy PM of India in 1977, Instead of PM of India. Dalit Community felt again deceived by the upper caste leaders. Babu Jagjivan Ram Ji took his last breath on 6 July 1986 & he left this world.

After that, his daughter Meera Kumari become Indian politician and former diplomat, minister, speaker of Lok sabha (lower chamber of the indian parliament and also contest the election of president of india but she was defeated by Ram Nath Kovind of the BJP.

Manyavar Kanshi Ram (15 March 1934)

Kanshi Ram, filled the Gap in the Indian political scenario and also known as Bahujan **Nayak** or **Manyavar** or **Saheb**, was an Indian  politician and social reformer who worked for the upliftment and political mobilisation of the Bahujans, the backward or lower caste people, including untouchable groups at the bottom of the caste system in India. Towards this end, Kanshi Ram founded Dalit Shoshit Samaj Sangharsh Samiti (DS-4), the All India Backward (SC, ST, OBC..) and Minorities Communities Employees' Federation (BAMCEF) in 1971 and the Bahujan Samaj Party (BSP) in 1984. However, he ceded leadership of the BSP to his protégé Behan Kumari Mayawati who has served four terms as Chief Minister of Uttar Pradesh. Kanshi Ram was born to a Ramdasia family of Chamar caste on 15th March 1934 in Ropar district, Punjab, India.

Kanshi Ram joined the Explosive Research and Development Laboratory office in Pune. At this time, he first experienced caste discrimination, and in 1964, he became a Social activist. Those who admire him point out that he was spurred to this after reading B.R. Ambedkar's book Annihilation of Caste and witnessing the discrimination against Dalit employees wishing to observe a holiday celebrating Ambedkar's birth. B. R. Ambedkar and his philosophy strongly inspired Kanshi Ram.

Kanshi Ram initially supported the Republican Party of India (RPI) but became disillusioned with its cooperation with the Indian National Congress. In 1971, he founded the All India SC, ST, OBC and Minority Employees Association, and in 1978 this became BAMCEF. This organisation aimed to persuade educated members of the Scheduled Castes, Scheduled Tribes, Other Backwards Classes and Minorities to support Ambedkarite principles. BAMCEF was neither political nor religious, and it had no aims to agitate for its purpose. Suryakant Waghmore says it appealed to "the class among the Dalits that was comparatively well-off, mostly based in urban areas and small towns working as government servants and partially alienated from their untouchable identities".

Later, in 1981, Kanshi Ram formed another social organisation, Dalit Shoshit Samaj Sangharsh Samiti (DSSSS, or DS4). He started his attempt to consolidate the Dalit vote, and in 1984 he founded the Bahujan Samaj Party (BSP). He fought his first election in 1984. He said the party would fight the first election to lose, the next to get noticed, and the third election to win. Then he represented the 11th Lok Sabha (1996-1998) from Hoshiarpur; and was again elected as a member of the Lok Sabha from Etawah in Uttar Pradesh. The BSP found success in Uttar Pradesh, initially struggling to bridge the divide between Dalits and Other Backward Classes, but later, under Mayawati's leadership, it bridged this gap.

Kumari Mayawati (DOB; 15-01-1956)

Kumari Mayawati is an Indian politician, well-educated, who served as the 1st female Dalit Sucessfull Chief Minister most populous state of Uttar Pradesh in India four terms from 1995 to 1995, 1997 to 1997, 2002 to 2003 and from 2007 to 2012. She was from weakest strata of Indian society to ruling elite serves as inspiration for millions of Indian who are still not free from Shakles of Casteism and discrimination.

Clearly, the above-said leader has done great work for the downtrodden / lower Society. But, still, even we are not achieving the goal as Satguru Ravidass Ji gave the message in the 15th Century about the welfare state where all human beings should live happily. Then **know about the master key that can open all the locks of fate, i.e. power and success by becoming the Ruler and by capturing Political Power.**

Part -2

By capturing Political Power

Why do we need to capture Political Power? The answer is clear, the reason behind the poverty, slavery, discrimination, lynching and casteism is due to the powerless Society. Without economic, social, and political power, the concept of Begampura will not be fulfilled. The idea of equality, freedom and democracy is meaningless. That's why we need to understand the way how to capture all the powers. For this, let's learn about the brief History of Indian civilization.

A brief history of Indian Civilisation

The Civilization of the Indus Valley & the Arrival of the Aryans is essential to know the history of the Indus Valley civilisation, how the Aryans conquered the Indian empire, and how they succeeded in making the slave the original native of India. Knowledge about History is necessary because **history grows your mind**. The history of Indian civilisation, as per the latest research, is that the **Indus Valley Civilization** sites were founded by the British Railway Crew in 1856, near the border of Nepal, in Afghanistan, on the coasts of India, and around Delhi, to name only a few locations. The Indus Valley Civilization is one of the oldest in the world, along with Mesopotamia and Egypt. It was famous for its great cities like Harappa, which were technologically advanced and highly cultured urban centres. The Indus Valley Civilization flourished between c. 7000 - c. 600 BCE and began to decline between c. 1900 - c. 1500 BCE, and the civilization began to decline.

In the early 20th century CE, this was thought to have been caused by an invasion of light-skinned peoples from the north known as Aryans, who conquered dark-skinned people defined by Western scholars as Dravidians. This claim, known as the Aryan Invasion Theory, has been discredited. The Aryans, whose ethnicity is associated with the Iranian Persians, are now believed to have migrated to the region.

The early Iranians self-identified as Aryans, meaning "noble", "free", or "civilized", About the arrival of the Aryans has also written by the first Prime Minister of India, Sh. Jawahar Lal Nehru in the **Discovery of India.**

The Indus Valley Civilization (also known as the Harappan Civilization or Harappan Culture. This civilization was highly advanced, as evidenced by Neolithic sites such as Mehrgarh, occupied before 7000 BCE, whose populace developed agricultural techniques, religious rituals, domestication of plants and animals, and produced impressive artistic works.

By c. 2600 BCE, the great cities of Harappa, Mohenjo-Daro, Ganeriwala, and over 1,000 others had risen, the ruins of which give evidence of advanced urban planning and technological skill. These cities had running water and a highly developed sewer and drainage system, which directed rainwater or waste toward fixtures on either side of the streets. Homes were constructed in such a way as to cut down on outside noises and were built with "wind catchers", which provided air conditioning within, a luxury not even Rome, at its height, developed. The people of the Indus Valley also created a writing system (as yet undeciphered), musical instruments, farming implements, and large, flat-bottomed boats. Ports were constructed with great warehouses for goods, and trade was conducted with several other nationalities, notably the people of Mesopotamia and Egypt.

Mohenjo-daro (Andrzej Nowojewski (CC BY-SA)

At some point between c. 1900 - c. 1500 BCE, the Indus Valley Civilization began to decline. Cities were abandoned, and people moved significantly toward the south of the subcontinent. This period of migration and change coincides with the development of Vedic thought and the so-called Vedic Period (c. 1500 - c. 500 BCE) when the Vedas, the sacred texts of Hinduism.

As written above, many Kings came to India, established their kingdoms, and ruled the country as per their religion and culture. They spread their religion/faith and were forced to convert to it and try to eliminate other religions.

Buddhism

Buddhism is an ancient Indian religion, which arose in and around the ancient Kingdom of Magadha (now in Bihar, India) and is based on the teachings of the Gautama Buddha, who was deemed a "Buddha" ("Awakened One"),

The practice of Buddhism as a distinct and organized religion lost influence after the Gupta reign (c.7th century CE), and the last state to support it, the Pala Empire, fell in the 12th century. By the end of the 12th

40

century, it had largely disappeared except for the Himalayan region and isolated remnants in parts of south India. However, since the 19th century, modern revivals of Buddhism have included; the Maha Bodhi Society, the Vipassana movement& the Dalit Buddhist movement spearheaded by B.R Ambedkar. There has also been a growth in Tibetan Buddhism with the arrival of the Tibetan diaspora and the Tibetan government in exile in India, following the Chinese annexation of Tibet in 1950.

B.R. Ambedkar delivering a speech during conversion, Nagpur, 14 Oct. 1956.

Deekshabhoomi monument, located in Nagpur, Maharashtra where B.R. Ambedkar converted to Buddhism in 1956 is the largest stuna in Asia.

In the 1950s, the Dalit political leader B. R. Ambedkar (1891-1956) Dalit Buddhist Movement was most successful in the Indian state of Maharashtra, which saw large-scale conversions. Ambedkar's "Neo Buddhism" included a strong element of social and political protest against Hinduism and the Indian caste system.

The conversion movement has generally been limited to specific social demographics, such as the Mahar caste of Maharashtra and the Jatavs. Although they have renounced Hinduism in practice, a community survey showed adherence to many traditions of the old faith, including endogamy, worshipping the traditional family deity etc.

Significant organizations of this movement are the Buddhist Society of India (the Bharatiya Bauddha Mahasabha) and the Triratna Buddhist Community (the Triratna Bauddha Mahasangha).

Nanda dynasty (C 343-321-BCE)

According to the Buddhist text, Mahabodhivamsa. In c. 322 BCE, Dhana Nanda lost his empire to Chandragupta Maurya after being defeated by him. The army attacked Dhana Nanda's capital but was soundly crushed and dissolved. Chandragupta and Chanakya assembled a new army and began seizing border settlements. They gradually proceeded to the Nanda capital of Pataliputra and assassinated Dhana Nanda.

Dhana Nanda's father, Mahapadma Nanda, was the son of a Shishunaga dynasty monarch. Mahapadma Nanda was the **first Shudra King** The Nanda period was considered significant in Indian history. One reason for this is that the Nanda monarchs established a competent administrative structure required to administer a vast empire. According to the Buddhist classic Maha Bodhi Vamsa, Dhana Nanda was the last emperor of ancient India's Nanda dynasty. After that, Chanakya's pupil, Chandragupta Maurya, was put on the throne, ultimately ending the Nanda Empire and ushering in the Mauryan Empire.

*****

42

Chapter - 6

Maurya Empire (C322-184 BCE)

Chandragupta Maurya

(322-297 BCE)

Founder of the first Indian United Empire

Chandragupta Maurya was an important figure in the history of India, laying the foundations of the first state to unite most of India. He created a new empire based on the principles of statecraft, built a large

army, and continued expanding the boundaries of his empire until ultimately renouncing it for an ascetic life in his final years. Prior to his consolidation of power, Alexander the Great had invaded the North-West Indian. Chandragupta defeated and conquered both the Nanda Empire, and the Greek satraps that were appointed or formed from Alexander's Empire in South Asia. He set out to conquer the Nanda Empire centered in Pataliputra, Magadha. Afterwards, Chandragupta expanded and secured his western border, where he was confronted by Seleucus I Nicator in the - SeleucidMauryan war. After two years of war, Chandragupta was considered to have gained the upper hand in the conflict and annexed satrapies up to the Hindu Kush. Instead of prolonging the war, both parties settled on a marriage treaty between Chandragupta and Seleucus I Nicator's daughter.

Chandragupta's empire extended throughout most of the Indian subcontinent, spanning from modern day Bengal to Afghanistan across North India as well as making inroads into Central and South India. Chandragupta's reign, and the Maurya Empire, set an era of economic prosperity, reforms, infrastructure expansions, and tolerance. Many religions thrived within his realms and his descendants' empire.

Buddhism, Jainism and Ajivika gained prominence alongside Vedic and Brahmanistic traditions, and minority religions such as Zoroastrianism and the Greek pantheon were respected. A memorial for Chandragupta Maurya exists on the Chandragiri hill along with a seventh-century hagiographic inscription.

Bindusara
(297-273 BCE)

 Bindusara, Known for his foreign diplomacy and crushed of Vidarbh revolt. Greatest emperor of dynasty. His son Kunala was blinded and died before his father. Ashoka was succeeded by his grandson. Also known for Kalinga war victory.

Ashoka
(268-232 BCE)

Ashoka his other names were Devanampiya (Sanskrit Devanampriya meaning Beloved of the Gods) and Piyadasi considered one of India's greatest emperors. He was born in 304 BC. His reign lasted from 268 BC to 232 BC when he died. At its zenith, Ashoka's empire stretched from Afghanistan in the west to Bangladesh in the east. It covered almost the whole Indian subcontinent except Kerala, Tamil Nadu, and modern-day Sri Lanka. Ashoka built many edicts all over India, including in present-day Nepal and Pakistan. His capital was at Pataliputra (Patna), and he had provincial capitals at Taxila and Ujjain.

Dashratha Maura
(232-224 BCE)

Grandson of Ashoka.

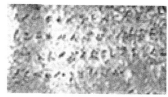

Samprati
(224-215 BCE)
Brother of Dasharatha.

Shalishuka
(215-202 BCE)

Devavarman
(202-195 BCE)

Shatadhanvan
(195-187 BCE)

The Mauryan Empire had shrunk by the time of his reign

Brihadratha
(187-184 BCE)

He was assassinated by his Commander-in-chief, Pushyamitra Shunga, in 185 BCE.

A Massacre (Killing of a large number of people at the same time in a violent and cruel way) of the Budhist and Shudras.

Brihadratha was the last ruler of the Maurya dynasty, dethroned (removing a monarch by killing them from power) by Pushyamitra Shunga in 185 BCE)

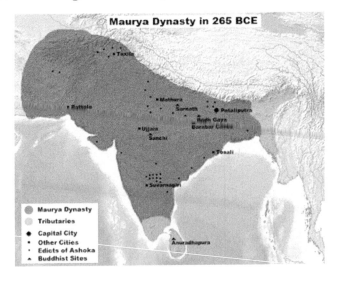

Shunga Empire (c. 185 – 73 BCE)

The last of the Shunga emperors was Devabhuti (83–73 BCE). He was assassinated by his minister **Vasudeva Kanva** and is said to have been overfond of the company of women.

The subsequent Kanvas then replaced the Shunga dynasty. Finally, the Kanva dynasty succeeded the Shungas around 73 BCE. **Kanva dynasty**, also called **Kanvayanas,** were the successors of the Shungas in the North Indian kingdom of Magadha, who ruled about

72–28 BCE like their predecessors. They were Brahmans in origin and have written their **Granth**, i.e., **The Vedas, Upanishads, Smritis, and Puranas, including the Ramayana and the Mahabharata, which are the Hindu Scriptures.**

Ram Raj as per the Ramayana

Pushyamitra Shunga, the Commander-in-chief of Brihadratha was Assassinated in 185 BCE. A Massacre (Killing a large number of people (Buddhists and Shudras) at the same time in a violent in a cruel way and an illusion has been created, (as per Buddhist literature) , i.e.:-

Rama killed Ravana and became the King. After becoming the King, there is another story in the Ramayana of Rama killing Shambuka. Some people seem to blame Rama because he wants only and without reason to kill Shambuka. But to blame Rama for killing Shambuka is to misunderstand the whole situation. Ram Raj was based on Chaturvarnya. As a king, Rama was bound to maintain Chaturvarnya. It was his duty; therefore, he killed Shambuka, the Shudra who had transgressed his class and wanted to be a Brahmin. This is the reason why Rama killed Shambuka. But this also shows that penal sanction was necessary for the maintenance of Chaturvarnya. That is why the Manu-Smriti prescribes such heavy sentences as cutting off the tongue or pouring of molten lead in the ears of the Shudra who recites or hears the Veda.

The following Empire has been Ruled the Country as mentioned below;-

- Gupta Empire (320 - 550 AD)
- Chola Empire (301 BC - 1279 AD)
- Chalukya Empire (543 - 1156 AD)
- Maratha Empire (1674 - 1820 AD)
- Vijayanagara Empire (1336 - 1660 AD)
- Mamluk dynasty (1206 - 1290 CE)
- Khalji dynasty (1290 - 1320 CE)

- • Tughlaq dynasty (1321 - 1414 CE)
- • Jaunpur Sultanate (1394 - 1479 CE)
- • Sayyid dynasty (1414 - 1451 CE)
- • Lodi dynasty (1451 - 1526 CE)

Sikandar Khan Lodi, born Nizam Khan, was an Afghan or a Turco-Afghan Sultan of the Delhi Sultanate between 1489 and 1517. He became ruler of the Lodi dynasty after the death of his father Bahlul Khan Lodi in July 1489.

There is a story regarding King Sikandar Lodhi and Saint Ravidass JI, Sikandar Lodhi converted a large number of Hindus to Islam. The Pandit saw Guru Ravidass Ji dressed as a Hindu (Brahmin) and reported to the King and King ordered his soldiers to arrest Satguru (Saint) Ravidass Ji and put him in prison. Satguru Ravidass Ji objected and revolt against the policies of the King and soon the King realised his mistake and begged an apology from Satguru Ravidass Ji. Sikander Lodhi asked Guru Ji about their wish then Satguru Ravidass Ji narrated the Hyme about the concept of State :

Aisa Chahu Raj Mai Jahan Miley Saban Ko Ann|
Sodh Bare Sab Sam Basse Ravidass Rahe Parsan||

(Satguru Ravidass JI)

King Sikandar Khan Lodhi has given the Status of Raj Guru to Satguru Ravidass Ji.

Chapter - 7

The Mughal Empire (1526 - 1857 AD)

In 1206 CE, the Islamic conquests made limited inroads into modern Afghanistan and Sindh as early as the 8th century, followed by the invasions of Mahmud Ghazni. The Delhi Sultanate was founded by Central Asian Turks who ruled a major part of the northern Indian subcontinent in the early 14th century but declined in the late 14th century and saw the advent of the Deccan sultanates. The wealthy Bengal Sultanate also emerged as a significant power, lasting over three centuries.

The Mughal dynasty was founded in **1526** when Babur, a Central Asian Muslim prince, followed the example of his ancestor Timur (d. 1405) and invaded the land he knew as Hindustan (the Indian subcontinent), victory over the Lodhi Sultan by Babur used 20 cannons to defeat an army twice the size of his own. But he died two years later, so it wasn't really Babur's leadership that sustained his dynasty. That success belonged to his grandson, who managed to expand Mughal territories and establish a highly efficient governance structure. Extensive commercial activity, both in trade and textile production, created great wealth. By the

49

early seventeenth century, Mughals governed one of the world's most populous and affluent empires in world history.

The early modern period began in the 16th century when the Mughal Empire conquered most of the Indian subcontinent. However, the Mughals suffered a gradual decline in the early 18th century, which provided opportunities for the Marathas, Sikhs, Mysoreans, Nizams, and Nawabs of Bengal to exercise control over large regions of the Indian subcontinent.

The Shudra community, which was at the bottom of the Hindu caste system, did not receive much attention or support from the Mughal rulers, who tended to focus on the interests of the elites.

Overall, the actions of the Mughal rulers towards the Shudra community were mixed. While some Mughal emperors did make efforts to improve the lives of the oppressed, many others did not prioritize their welfare and perpetuated systems of oppression and inequality. But there is no dought that the **Saints/Bhagti movement** has been started in their regime and can challenge the Brahminical system and also raise objections against Muslim rulers.

The Mughal emperors were among India's greatest patrons of art, responsible for some of the country's most spectacular monuments, like the palaces at Delhi, Agra, and Lahore (in present-day Pakistan) and the famous mausoleum, the Taj Mahal.

The 19th and last Mughal emperor, Bahadur Shah II, was deposed by the British in 1858, and the British Raj replaced the Mughal dynasty.

*****

Chapter - 8

Bhakti (Saint) movement

India's Bhakti (Saint) movement emerged during the medieval period, roughly between the 7th and 17th centuries. It was a devotional movement that emphasized the love and devotion of individuals towards a personal form of God or a divine entity. The campaign responded to the time's prevalent religious and social conditions, and it sought to bring about spiritual and social reform.

There were several reasons for the emergence of the Bhakti movement in India. One of the main reasons was the growing disillusionment of the masses with the existing religious and social orders. The traditional Indian society was dominated by the Brahmins, who controlled the religious and social systems. This led to the exclusion and marginalization of the lower castes and women.

The Bhakti movement challenged this hierarchical system and offered a more inclusive and egalitarian approach to spirituality. The influence of Islamic Sufi saints also played a role in the development of the Bhakti movement. The Sufis emphasized the personal experience regarding God and rejected the rigid dogmas and rituals of organized religion. This resonated with the Bhakti movement's focus on individual devotion and personal experience of the divine.

The Bhakti movement also responded to the challenges posed by foreign invasions and the breakdown of political and social order. The movement offered a spiritual and social alternative to the prevailing chaos and uncertainty.

The Bhakti movement gave rise to several prominent poets and saints who spread the message of devotion and love toward God. These included figures like Shiromani Sant Ravidass ji, Sant Kabir ji, Guru Nanak Dev ji, Sant Namdev, Sant Tirlochan ji, Sant Sadna ji, Sant Sadana ji, Sant Mirabai, and, among others. The movement profoundly impacted Indian society, shaping the religious and cultural landscape of the country.

As a social movement, the Bhakti movement in Karnataka, and indeed everywhere in India, challenged caste hierarchy, raised voice against Muslim Ruler and Brahmanical caste System and emphasized the individual's direct connection to god and the possibility of salvation for all through good deeds and simple living. As a literary movement,

Saint Sadhna ji

Sant Sadhna was born in 1180 at Vill. Sehwan in Hyderabad. Died at Sirhind, Fatehgarh Sahib. Sant Sadhna's teachings emphasized the importance of self-realization and service to society. He believed that spirituality and social welfare were interconnected and that spiritual progress was not possible without a commitment to serving others as a means of achieving inner peace and clarity and to use their spiritual knowledge to help those in need.

Saint Sadhna ji, also called Sadhna Qasai, was a north Indian poet, saint, mystic and one of the devotees whose hymn was incorporated into Guru Granth Sahib. Venerated in the region of Punjab, among Sikhs and Ravidassia, most preachers widely quote his devotional hymn. His one hymn is present in Adi Granth Sahib, in Raga Bilaval. The followers of Bhagat Sadhna are called Sadhna Panthis. His only memorial is a mosque at Sirhind, where he died.

Saint Namdev Ji
(1270-1350)

Saint Namdev was a prominent Indian saint and poet who lived in the 13th century. He was a part of the Bhakti movement that emphasized personal devotion to God and challenged the rigid caste system of Hindu society. Namdev was born in a low-caste family in Maharashtra, India. He has composed numerous poems and hymns in praise of God. His devotional songs were popular among all sections of society and helped spread the message of the Bhakti movement.

Namdev's teachings emphasized the importance of devotion, love, and service to God. He believed that God could be experienced through pure devotion and that the caste system was a barrier to this experience. He was a strong advocate of social equality and rejected the idea of caste-based discrimination.

Namdev's life and teachings had a significant impact on Indian society. His poems and hymns are still sung and recited in religious gatherings, and he is regarded as a revered saint by many. His teachings continue to inspire people to live a life of devotion, love, and service to God.

.   Namdev was also recognised in the North Indian traditions of the Dadu Panthis, Kabir Panthis and Sikhs. Some hymns of Namdev are included in the Guru Granth Sahib.

Saint Trilochan Ji

Saint Trilochan ji was born in 1269, District. Solapur, Maharashtra, as per Mahankosh. He was a celebrated medieval Indian saint and one of the devotees whose hymns are present in Guru Granth Sahib, the holy book of Sikhs.

Saint Trilochan's teachings were based on universal brotherhood, love, and devotion to God. He emphasized the importance of leading a moral and virtuous life. He spent most of his life traveling across northern India, spreading his message of love and peace.

Ravidassia community also acknowledge Satguru Trilochan and preach his teaching and thought, as Satguru Ravidass Ji, in his holy hymn, believes and admires Satgur Trilochan as a great devotee among Kabir, Sadhna, Sain, and Namdev. The sacred book of Ravidass' teachings, the

!'Amritbani Guru Ravidass Ji", and many Ravidassia temples have published this Granth. Dera Sach Khand Ballan of Jalandhar, Punjab, has announced the objectives of the Ravidassia religion and written to propagate the Bani and teachings of Satguru Ravidass Ji, Bhagwan Balmiki Ji, Satguru Namdev, Satguru Kabir Ji, Satguru Trilochan Ji, Satguru Sain Ji, and Satguru Sadhna Ji.

Saint Sain Ji
(1343-1440, aged 96–97)

Saint Sain Ji was a religious figure who lived at the end of the fourteenth and the beginning of the fifteenth century. His name was known in every house due to his devotion to god. Bhagat Sain was a barber of the royal court of Raja Ram, king of Rewa. The general view is that he was born in Punjab but toured all over India, where he may have served both the kings of Bandhavgarh and Bidar. 6 December is celebrated as his birth anniversary in Punjab. Now a Gurudwara and a holy tank (*Sarovar*) stand where he used to meditate in Partabpura, Punjab. He was also well-known in Maharashtra, Rajasthan, and other parts of India.

Shiromani Saint Satguru Ravi Dass ji
(1377-1528 AD)(1433-1584 Vikrmi-Sambat)

Satguru Ravidass Ji was born into a family of leather workers (chamar) in Varanasi.

Satguru Ravidass Ji spoke of the need for a casteless society. In one of his famous hymn, Satguru Ravi Dass says of "Begumpura"—"a place with no pain, no taxes, no wrong doing, worry, terror or torture (translated by Hawley and Juergen Meyer in Songs of the Saints of India). In this verse and in many others, Satguru Ravidass Ji gave voice to lower-caste pain at Brahminical society's treatment of them. The Ravidassia community that continues to flourish today is evidence of his appeal's everlasting nature.

While Ravi Dass, Kabir, and Nanak spoke of the formless god (nirgun bhakti), Meerabai (1498-1546) from Rajasthan composed and sang devotional verses in praise of her Guru Ravi Dass. Meera's intense devotion to her Guru Ravi Dass, in defiance of patriarchal norms, was rebellious. The entire Bani of Satguru Ravidass ji has been written in the Holy Granth of Amritbani.

Saint Kabir Das ji
(1398–1518)

Saint Kabir Das Ji were a 15th-century Indian mystic poet and saint whose writings influenced Hinduism's Bhakti movement, and his verses are found in Sikh scripture Guru Granth Sahib.

He was a revolutionary Saint and raised his voice against the present Muslim Ruler and Brahmanical system. Satguru Kabir Ji has written in his hymn that: - **"Santan mein Ravidass Sant Hain" And** more about Satguru Ravidass Ji.

Satguru Kabir Ji condemned all the superstition and anti-human system. Kabir ji was also a humanitarian. According to a stanza by Kabir Das, his religion is the right way to live life. He is neither a Hindu nor a Muslim by religion. Kabir Das ji has been quite abusive of religious rituals. He has also opposed the evil practices going on in the name of religion. The birth of Kabir Das was contemporary with the founding of Sikhism, which is why his influence is also seen in Sikhism. Kabir had to face opposition from Hindus and Muslims many times during his lifetime.

One of the famous stanza of Sant Kabir Das Ji

Soora So Pehchaniye Jo Lare Deen Ke Het|
Purja Purja Kat Marai Kabhoon Na Chaade Khet||

Means:- He is a warrior who fights in defense of truthful, moral, and pure actions, he may be cut apart piece by piece, but he never leaves the field of battle.

Guru Nanak Dev Ji (1469-1539)

Guru Nanak, the founder of Sikhism, came from a Hindu family in a village populated by both Hindus and Muslims. At 13, the Guru declined the sacred thread at his coming-of-age ceremony. Some years later, he vanishing for three days, then Guru ji returned to his family with revelation from God.

Guru Nanak and other Sikh Gurus emphasized bhakti ('love', 'devotion', or 'worship'), and taught that the spiritual life and secular householder life are intertwined. From the Sikh perspective, the everyday world is part of an infinite reality, where increased spiritual awareness leads to increased and vibrant participation in the everyday world. Guru Nanak described living an "active, creative, and practical life" of "truthfulness, fidelity, self-control, and purity" as being higher than the metaphysical truth.

Nanak's teaching have been put into practice through popular tradition in three ways:

Kirat Karo

- (ਕਿਰਤ ਕਰੋ 'work honestly'): Earn an honest living without exploitation or fraud; and

Vand Shhako

- (ਵੰਡ ਛਕੋ, 'share & consume'): Share with others, help those who are in need, so you may eat together;

Naam Japo

- (ਨਾਮ ਜਪੋ, 'recite His name'): Meditate on God's name, so to feel His presence and control the five thieves of the human personality.

He said that despite religion, caste, and gender, everyone should seek well for others and only then one can have that goodness back in return. "Nanak Naam Chardi Kala Tere Bhane Sarbat da bhala", which means "Nanak with your name and blessings, may everyone in the world prosper and be in peace."

*****

Chapter - 9

Sikh Empire (1801 - 49 CE)

Before the study of the Sikh Empire, we should learn about Sikhism. Sikhism is based on the spiritual teachings of many Saints and Gurus. Guru Nanak Dev Ji collected Bani of different Saints, which has preserved in the Guru Granth Sahab Ji. After Guru Nanak Dev Ji, the following Guru had predecessors, as mentioned below:

	**First Guru:** Shri Guru Nanak Sahib Guru Nanak Sahib (the First Nanak, the founder of Sikhism) was born on 15th April, 1469 at Rai - Bhot - di Talwandi in the present district of Shekhupura (Pakistan)		**Second Guru:** Shri Guru Angad SahibGuru Angad Sahib, (Bhai Lahna ji) was born in the village named Harike in Ferozepur district in Punjab, on Vaisakh Vadi Ist, (5th Vaisakh) Samvat 1561, (March 31, 1504)
	**Third Guru:** Shri Guru Amardas SahibGuru Amardas Sahib, the Third Nanak was born at village Basarke Gillan in Amritsar district on Vaisakh Sudi 14th, (8th Jeth), Samvat 1536 (5th May 1479)		**Fourth Guru:** Shri Guru Ramdass Sahib Ji Guru Ramdas Sahib (Jetha ji) was born at Chuna Mandi, Lahore (in Pakistan), on Kartik Vadi 2nd, (25th Assu) Samvat 1591 (September 24, 1534)
	Fifth Guru: Shri Guru Arjan Sahib Ji Guru Arjan Sahib, the youngest son of Guru Ramdas Sahib and Mata Bhani J was born at Goindwal Sahib on Vaisakh Vadi 7th, (19th Vaisakh) Samvat 1620 (April 15, 1563)		**Sixth Guru:** Shri Guru Hargobind Sahib JiGuru Hargobind Sahib was born at village Guru Ki Wadah (district Amritsar) on Harh Vadi 7th (21 Harh), Samvat 1652 (19th June, 1595)
	**Seventh Guru:** Shri Guru Har Rai Sahib Ji Guru Hargobind Sahib, before his departure for heavenly abode, nominated has grand son, Har Rai Ji at the tender age of 14, as his successor (Seventh Nanak), on 3rd March, 1644		**Eight Guru:** Shri Guru Har Krishan Sahib Ji Guru Harkrishan Sahib was born on Sawan Vadt 10, (8 Sawan), Bikrami Samvat 1713, (July 7, 1656) at Kiratpur Sahib
	Ninth Guru: Shri Guru Tegh Bahadur Sahib JiGuru Tegh Bahadur Sahib was born on Vaisakh Vadi 5, (5 Vaisakh), Bikrami Samvat 1678, (1st April, 1621) in the holy city of Amritsar in a house known as Guru ke Mahal		**Tenth Guru:** Shri Guru Gobind Singh Sahib Ji The tenth and the last Guru or Prophet-teacher of the Sikh faith, was born Gobind Rat Sodhi on Poh Such 7th. 23rd Poh 1723 Bikrami Samvat (22 December 1666) at Patna, in Bihar.

Guru Granth Sahib Ji

Bhai Gurdas, who was initiated by Guru Amardas and who wrote the Guru Granth Sahib at the 5th Guru Arjan's dictation, the Bani has been collected by Guru Nanak from the Saints. After the death of the tenth Guru, Guru Gobind Singh, the Sikh scripture, Guru Granth Sahib, became the literal embodiment of the eternal, impersonal Guru, where the scripture's word serves as the spiritual guide for Sikhs.

Guru Arjan Dev Ji compiled Guru Granth Sahab and Guru ji was torched and he was assassinated by Muslim Ruler then the 6th Guru Hargobind Ji adapted sword, thus, he began the militarization of the Sikh.

Guru Tegh Bahadur was the ninth Guru of the Sikhs, following the path laid down by the first Guru of the Sikhs, Guru Nanak Dev. He has composed 115 texts. When Kashmiri Pandits and other Hindus were forcibly converted to Islam, Guru Tegh Bahadur opposed it. In 1675 AD, he was beheaded in front of the Mughal ruler Aurangzeb because he did not accept Islam.

Guru Gobind Singh Ji (1666-1708)
Born: 22 Dec. 1666, Patna City.

The life example and leadership of tenth Guru Gobind Singh have been a historical importance to the Sikhs. Institutionalized the Khalsa (literally, Pure Ones), who played the key role in protecting the Sikhs long after his death.

The creation of the Khalsa in 1699 was the most dynamic master stroke in converting ordinary Sikhs from lower strata of society into Sant Sipahis where the saint aspect guided them to be pious in nature and at the same time valiant soldiers in the field. It seems to be an admixture in Miri and Piri for every soldier to a limited extent. The integration of the temporal and spiritual aspects has been the most significant contribution of the Sikh Gurus to the totality of the Sikh way of life, such as during the nine invasions of Panjab and the holy war led by Ahmad Shah Abdali from Afghanistan between 1747 and 1769. And last Guru Ji was seriously injured by the attack with nife and breathed his last **on** 7th October 1708,

Takhat Sachkhand Shri Hazur Abchal Nagar Sahib, Nanded, Maharastra. Some important quotations have been said by Guru Ji:

Raj Bina Nahin Dharam Chale Hain|
Dharam Bina Sab Dalle Malle Hain ||

This means:- that without political power, Dharam does not prosper, and without Dharam, the society remains an admixture of hoch poch.

Koi Kisi Ko Raj Na De Hae |
Jo Lai Hai Nij Bal Sit Lai Hae ||

This means that nobody gives self-rule as a gift to another, it is to be seized through their own strength.

Guru Gobind Singh Ji fought for justice and against the cruel ruler and for humanity, as well as for Sikh Empire.

Shabad has written for Boom the Power & Encourage the soldiers fight fearlessly.

Deh Siva Bar Mohe Eh-hey |
Subh Karman Te Kabhu Na Taro ||
Na Daro Arr Seo Jab Jaye Laro|
Nischey Kar Apni Jit Karo ||
Arr Sikh Ho Apne He Mann Ko|
Eh Laalach Hou Gun Tau Ucharo ||
Jab Aav Ki Audh Nidan Bane|
Att He Rann Me Tabh Joojh Maro ||

Mean :-O Power of Akaal, give me this boom. May I never ever shirk from doing good deeds. That I shall not fear when I go into combat. And with determination, I will be victorious. That I may teach myself this greed alone, to speak only of thy (Almighty Lord, Baheguru). Praises. And when the last day of my life comes, I may die on the might of the battle field.

Or "Give me strength, O Lord of the Sword, to embrace death

63

with joy. May my mind remain steadfast in the remembrance of Your Name, and may I never waver from performing good deeds."

This Shabad is often recited as a prayer for protection and strength and is commonly associated with the Sikh martial tradition. And also called **Sikh National Anthem.**

Guru Gobind Singh fought 13 battles against the Mughal Empire and the kings of Siwalik Hills.

Before this, Shri Guru Teg Bahadur Ji, father of Guru Gobind Singh ji, the ninth guru of the Sikhs, who stood up against forcible conversions by the Mughals, and was beheaded/executed on the orders of Aurangzeb in 1675. Bhai Jaita Ji, who was a Dalit, took the head of Guru Tegh Bahadur Ji to Anandpur Sahib, and Guru Gobind Singh Ji called him "Rangreta Guru Ka Beta". Guru Gobind Singh's four sons, also called Chaar Sahibzaade (the four princes), were killed during Guru Ji`s lifetime – the elder two in a battle with the Mughals, and the younger two executed by the Mughal governor of Sirhind.

During the Battle of Chamkaur, Guru Gobind Singh Ji gave his Kalgi (Crown) and dress (Chola) to Baba Sangat Singh Ji before leaving the Fort; Baba Sangat Singh Ji belonged to Ravidassia (Chamar) and died in the Battle at Chamkaur Sahib. Many others have fought on the battlefield with bravery, given their lives, and created history.

Giani Ditt Singh(Ravidassia) was a historian, scholar, poet, editor, and eminent Singh Sabha reformer. Singh wrote over 70 books on Sikhism, the most famous of which is Khalsa Akhbar. His *"Dayanand naal mera Samvaad"* and *Durga Parbodh* are considered major texts of Sikh philosophy.

Sikh Empire under King Ranjit Singh

Maharaja Ranjit Singh has governed the Sikh State North-western regions of the Indian subcontinent. The empire, based around the Punjab region, existed from 1799 to 1849 under the leadership of Maharaja Ranjit Singh from an array of autonomous Punjabi Missals of the Sikh Confederacy. Central Punjab, the provinces of Multan, Kashmir, and the Peshawar Valley to his empire. At its peak, in the 19th century, the empire extended from the Khyber Pass in the west to Kashmir in the north, to Sindh in the south, running along the Sutlej river to Himachal in the east.

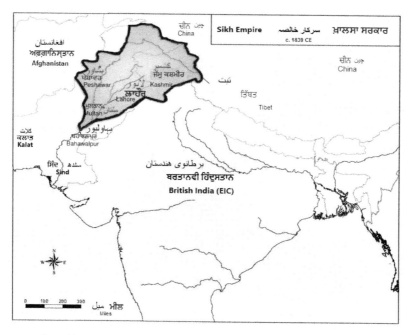

The Sikh empire at its greatest geographical extent, ca. 1839

The foundation of the Sikh Empire can be traced to as early as 1707, the year of Aurangzeb's death and the start of the downfall of the Mughal Empire. The Dal Khalsa was formed by Guru Gobind Singh, led expeditions against them and the Afghans in the west. Each of these component armies controlled different areas and cities. However, in the period from 1762 to 1799, Sikh commanders of the misls appeared to be coming into their own as independent.

During the Sikh Empire, the Sikhs ruled over parts of present-day India and Pakistan, including the Punjab, Kashmir, and parts of Himachal Pradesh, Haryana, and Rajasthan. The empire peaked under Maharaja Ranjit Singh, known for his military conquests and patronage of the arts and architecture.

Shri Harmandir Sahib (Golden Temple)

The Harmandir Sahib is the prominent pilgrimage site of Sikhism. In 1581, Guru Arjan Dev initiated its construction and the Harminder Sahib took 8 years to complete. Ranjit Singh rebuilt it in marble and copper in 1809 and overlaid the sanctum with gold foil in 1830.

<u>Maharaja Ranjit Singh</u> (1780-1839)

Maharaja Ranjit Singh consolidated many parts of northern India into an empire. He primarily used his Sikh Khalsa Army, which he trained in European military techniques and equipped with modern military technologies. Ranjit Singh proved himself to be a master strategist and selected well-qualified generals for his army. He continuously defeated the Afghan armies and successfully ended the Afghan-Sikh Wars. In stages, he added central Punjab, the provinces of Multan and Kashmir, and the Peshawar Valley to his empire.

.   At its peak, in the 19th century, the empire extended from the Khyber Pass in the west to Kashmir in the north, to Sindh in the south, running along the Sutlej river to Himachal in the east. After the death of Ranjit Singh, the empire weakened, leading to conflict with the British East India Company. The hard-fought First Anglo-Sikh War and Second Anglo-Sikh War marked the downfall of the Sikh Empire, making it among the last areas of the Indian subcontinent to be conquered by the British.

During the Mughal empire, the life of oppressed and poor peoples was not so good, and the Brahmanical system was based on the caste system that tortured human beings. Then social reformers and saints preached against discrimination and united with each other. Due to this Unity, the Mughal empire became weak, and Sikhism came into force and became the Ruler and during that period British came into power and captured all Indian states.

*****

Chapter - 10

British Empire (1858–1947)

The East India Company came to India as traders in spices, an essential commodity in Europe back then as it was used to preserve meat. They also primarily traded in silk, cotton, indigo dye, tea, and opium. They landed in the Indian subcontinent on August 24, 1608, at the port of Surat.

The Mughal emperor Jahangir granted a Farman to Captain William Hawkins, permitting the English to erect a factory at Surat in 1613. Then, in 1615, Thomas Roe, the Ambassador to James I, got an imperial Farman from Jahangir to trade and establish factories all across the Mughal empire. After that British Empire was the rule of the British Crown on the Indian subcontinent; it is also called Crown rule in India or Direct rule in India. British rule started in India slowly but surely, and the East India Company transformed from a trading company to a ruling one. However, the powers of the East India Company kept growing till 1858, when it was dissolved after the Revolt of 1857, and **the British Crown took direct control of India to begin British rule.**

After that, Indians raised their demand for freedom, and many revolutionary organizations revolted against the British Government. Then Britain decided to leave India in a hurry **because they feared that if the mutiny spread to the army and police, there would be a large-scale killing of Britishers all over India.** Hence Britain decided to transfer power at the earliest, and Britain withdrew from India in 1947. During World War Two,

In the British Raj, the **Britishers allowed the Shudras and untouchables to come and get an education in their school, college, and Universities and can get treatment from their Hospitals even though Shudras could travel on the train, which was started by the British Government in India.**

They have to make rules to stop the old traditions against

humanity. **British Rule was not bad for the Shudras and the untouchable community.**

When the Britishers left the India, several socio-religious organizations came into being at that time.

- Muslims set up the All India Muslim League in 1906.

- The Hindu Mahasabha and Hindu revolutionaries sought to represent Hindu interests.

- Sikhs founded the Shiromani Akali Dal in 1920.

- However, Indian National Congress, founded in 1885, attempted to keep a distance from the socio-religious movements and identity politics.

- During this time, nobody was the Godfather of Shudras, who had long been Enslaved and untouchable by the Brahmanical system.

- The only Baba Shahab, Dr. Bhim Rao Ambedkar, was fighting for the rights of the Shudras and untouchables. After great efforts, Baba Sahab succeeded in getting the rights for Shudras and Scheduled Castes (the official name given in India to the lowest caste, considered `untouchable` in orthodox Hindu scriptures and practice) and writing the Indian Constitution. After Independence, Shudras/Scheduled Caste has also given equal rights. But unfortunately, even today, there is discrimination against them, and they are struggling to get equal rights, i.e., Social, Economic, and Social Justice, even though they seek to power to get their lost empire.

- Social Reforms: British Rule in India had done various social activities for the country, for instance, the **abolition of The Sati Pratha** and introduction of the **Widow Remarriage Act of 1856**, the **Child marriage restraint Act, the Act against child labour and many other acts for improving the social tradition and custom for the betterment of humanity.**

- The British introduced modern technologies such as railways, telegraphs, and modern medicine, which helped to transform India's economy and infrastructure.

- The British established a modern system of education, which led to the growth of a new middle class and helped to create a more educated and cosmopolitan Indian society.

- The British played a crucial role in unifying India, consolidating a large and diverse country under a single administration.

There are also many examples of British Rulers who exploited the Indians and committed many atrocities during their regime.

The turning point was also the Massacre of Amritsar on April 13, 1919, in which British troops fired on a large crowd of unarmed Indians in an open space known as the Jallianwala Bagh in Amritsar in the Punjab region.

Many Freedom fighters had killed, and Sardar Bhagat Singh, age 23, Sukhdev, age 23, and Rajguru, age 22, were hanged on March 23, 1931. There are many other reasons why the British Rulers have to leave India.

The British imposed a highly exploitative economic system on India, with the extraction of resources and wealth to Britain leaving many Indians in poverty and hardship.

The British enforced discriminatory laws and policies and imposition of a tax that affected the poorest in society the most.

The overall impact of British rule on India remains a subject of debate and controversy.

This period also saw the emergence of several powerful Hindu states, notably Vijayanagara and Rajput states, such as Mewar. The 15th century saw the advent of Sikhism. From the mid-18th century to the mid-19th century, the East India Company gradually annexed large regions of India. India was afterwards ruled directly by the British Crown in the British Raj. After World War I, a nationwide struggle for independence has launched by the Indians.

Later, the All-India Muslim League has advocate for a separate Muslim-majority nation-state. The British Indian Empire was partitioned in August 1947 into the Dominion of India and the Dominion of Pakistan, each gaining its seprate independence.

The fate of Shudras (untouchables), Scheduled caste/ Scheduled Tribes, was in the hands of Baba Sahab B.R. Ambedkar Ji. Because Baba Sahab fought for the rights of the Shudras, and he succeeded in getting their rights. He wrote the Constitution, which has adopted on 26 Jan 1950.

The **"Battle of Koregaon"** was a significant event in the history of India that took place on January 1, 1818, near the village of Koregaon in present-day Maharashtra, India. The battle was fought between the British East India Company's forces and the Peshwa Baji Rao II's army, which was supported by a large number of Maratha warriors.

The British forces consisted mainly of Mahar Dalit soldiers, considered low-caste and discriminated against by the upper-caste Maratha community.

Despite being outnumbered and outgunned, the British forces, led by Captain Francis Staunton, were able to hold off the Maratha army for almost an entire day. The victory was considered a significant achievement for the British and the Mahar soldiers, who were recognized for their bravery and loyalty.

The Battle of Koregaon is still remembered and celebrated by the Mahar community in India as a symbol of their struggle against caste discrimination and oppression. It has become an important part of Indian history and a source of inspiration for many social and political movements in the country

Ad-Dharmi movement

Ad-Dharmi movement was started by Babu Mangoo Ram Mugowalia ji. He was born in 1886 in a Chamar family at Vill. Muggowal, District Hoshiarpur, Punjab Province, British India. He was an Indian freedom fighter and Politician from Punjab who started the Ad-Dharam movement, which also helped to Baba Sahab movement. In 1925, after returning from the US, Babu Mangoo Ram began to teach in a primary school in his home village of Mugowal, which he named Ad-Dharm School. It was the same school where Babu Mangu Ram first convened the meeting that formally launched the Ad Dharam Movement. The movement's establishment was to raise their voice against society, which put Dalits at the bottom of the social structure. It was a glorious step by Dalits to attain equality in a caste-laden society. Babu Mangu Ram pioneered the Dalit movement in North India through the Ad-Dharm Movement.

That is the brief History of the Rulers who Rules in India. The change is the law of nature. Dalit History and Slavery have also changed their character. So before knowing how to get power, every one should know about casteism and slavery and their effects on humanity. And how to come out from slavery and casteism, which is very important to understand the process of slavery and casteism.

*****

Chapter - 11

Slavery and Casteism

First, know and understand slavery and casteism minutely, and why it has not been abolished till now. Thereofre, some examples and stories can help to come out of this **Sin**.

Slavery is a condition in which one human being is owned by another. A slave was considered by law as property, or chattel, and was deprived of most of the rights ordinarily held by free persons in modern slavery today - more than ever before - as poverty, conflict and crises fuel the growing global slave trade. From men made to work in factories, farms and fishing boats and women forced to sell sex to people exploited for their organs and children sent to beg or forced to marry, human trafficking is one of the fastest-growing criminal enterprises. North Korea, Eritrea and Burundi are estimated to have the world's highest rates of modern-day slavery, with India, China and Pakistan home to the largest number of victims. People can be trafficked for various forms of exploitation, such as prostitution, forced labour, begging, criminality, domestic servitude, forced marriage and organ removal. India is home to the largest number of slaves globally.

A civil relationship whereby one person has absolute power over another and controls his life, liberty, and fortune.

Type of Slavery

Historically, there have been many different types of slavery in the world. However, in modern times, there are generally considered to be two main types of slavery:

1. Traditional slavery: This refers to the classic form of slavery, where people are considered property and are bought and sold like objects. This type of slavery has been largely abolished in most parts of the world.

2. Modern slavery: This refers to the more contemporary forms of

73

slavery, such as forced labor, human trafficking, debt bondage, and other forms of exploitation. Unfortunately, modern slavery still exists in many parts of the world, with an estimated 40 million people currently being held in some form of slavery.

A) Chattel Slavery

Physical Slavery, Owne as human chattel just as an animal, dog, pig, cow, horse etc.

B) Bonded Labour

Bonded labor, also known as debt bondage and servant, happens when people give themselves into slavery as security against a loan or when they inherit a debt from a relative.

Bonded labour is prohibited in India by law vide Articles 21 and 23 of the Constitution. A specific law to prohibit the practice was legislated only in 1976 known as the Bonded Labour System (Abolition) Act.

In modern India after independence, the Government have not succeeded in abolishing this evil and there are many parts of India where bounded labour still exists.

According to the Ministry of Labor and Employment of the Government of India, there are **over 3,00,000** bonded labourers in India, with a majority of them in the states of Tamil Nadu, Karnataka, and Odisha.

C) <u>Forced Labour (Siri)</u>

Labour that villagers were forced to contribute without any payment was called Siri or Begar. It was a system of forced labor practiced in India in which people were compelled to perform unpaid work for rich people or By higher caste people class.

D) <u>Mental Slavery</u>

Mental Slavery is more dangerous than the other type of slavery. A mental slave is someone who suspends his intellectual faculties and subjugates himself to the will and beliefs and attitudes of another person or group. Mental slavery is the inability to view events, or one's self, objectively. A mental slave will not apply his brain to evaluate what he is being told, to discover what is true and rational; mental slaves are in the habit of accepting and believing what is told to them, whether it makes sense or not. Often, the mental slave does not even stop to ask himself whether what is being said makes sense or not; what is important is that my side said it. And then if the other side says something, the mental slave is conditioned to reject it as being nonsense, or self-serving.

These are not thinking people who weigh the issues and make reasoned choices. The slang which describes many of them is profoundly accurate: they are 'die-hearted' - their hearts are quite dead! If their party put up as a candidate a black dog or a monkey, they will vote for him or her. And manifestos and political debates will be lost on these diehard, unthinking, robotic party revelers.

Satguru Ravidass Ji said about slavery that:

Pradhinta Pap Hai Jan Lehu Re Meet|
Ravidass Das Pradin Soun Kaun Karai Hai Preet|| ||193||

Mean: That Ravidass says enslavement is a sin. O, friend! You should understand this important point because no one loves a slave man; we should know that slavery is a "**Sin**".

Casteism

Caste System in India & its Origin

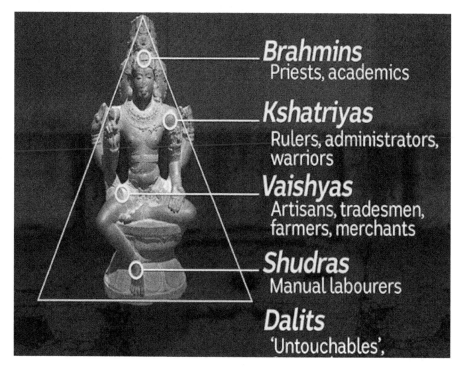

The caste system is a way of dividing society into hereditary classes. The caste system in India **originated with the arrival of the Aryans in India around 1,500 BC.** The caste system was called the **Verna and Jati**, the varna system in Vedic society (c. 1100 – c. 500 BCE). The purpose was to distribute responsibilities among the people, **these four classes originated from Brahma, the Hindu god of creation.** (Rg Veda-Hindu religious theory/scripture)

Varna:-Varna is a Sanskrit word that is translated as 'class'. **Varna is an ancient division with origin in the Vedas** (the oldest texts of Hinduism). According to the Rig Veda, the first man, Purush used his body to create a human society: Brahmins came from Purush's head, Kshatriyas came from Purush's arms, Vaishyas from his thighs, and Shudras from Purush's feet.

Jati:- Jati is from the Sanskrit root jaha meaning to be born. A jati describes a group or community that has generic hereditary characteristics. A person's jati determined his/her occupation and status, each varna contains many jatis. There are more than **3,000 jatis.**

Brahmins:- Highest Caste in India. They also had key positions in science, business, and government even though they are 5% of India's population.

Kshatriyas:- Second Highest of the Four Varnas: their main occupations are warriors and rulers. Kshatriyas traditionally learn weaponry and warfare, **The Kshatriyas had wealth and power** and were permitted material indulgence like eating meat, and many also enjoyed alcoholic drinks. The Kshatriyas make up around 4% of India's population and are mainly located in the north of India.

Vaishya:- Third Highest of the Four Varnas. Vaishyas mainly control commercial and agricultural occupations. They become strong economically because of their close relation to commerce and many become traders, merchants, landowners, and money-lenders.

Sudras:- Lowest Fourth is the lowest caste i.e. laborers, Servants and craftsmen, nearly half of India's population.

Dalits/Ashoot ("Untouchables") The caste system did not consider the **Dalits — Ashoot, the "untouchables"**, people who had no jati classification. Outside of the caste system, hateful people.

Caste is Hereditary. In general, the caste of your parents determines your caste, and your caste determines the caste of your children.

In general, upper castes were prohibited from having contact with lower castes. The upper castes lived in the centre of society, while the lower castes lived in the periphery. Water wells were not shared, Brahmins would not accept food or drink from Shudras, etc. **Vegetarians and abstainers had a higher status than meat-eaters.**

Lower castes were given the status of **Scheduled Castes (SC),** and **Scheduled Tribes (ST),** and the slightly higher-ranked-but-still-poor were called **Other Backward Classes (OBC).** The Indian government introduced many policies of positive discrimination such as quotas in government, employment, and education for members of lower castes. **Casteism has long been deeply rooted in the hearts of Indians,** so it is hard to change it in a short time. India is still a long way from completely abolishing the caste system.

After Independence, equal rights has given in the constitution and many people have become doctors, lawyers, and professors, changing the destiny of their ancestors, inter-caste marriages are becoming more common. Some have gone abroad and made big achievements in foreign countries.

The Indian Constitution has outlawed the practice of Untouchability and the Indian Government has established special quotas in schools and Parliament to aid the lowest jatis. Caste discrimination is not permitted in gaining employment and access to educational and other opportunities.

But this does not mean that caste is illegal or has faded away. Caste groups as political pressure groups work very well in a democratic system. Caste may provide psychological support that people seem to need. Economists and political scientists are finding that caste is no real barrier to economic development or political democracy.

The high-caste people made them lead wretched life. **This caste system made mobility of anyone impossible, it restricted someone in the caste to follow only the prescribed duties.** Basically, the caste system made the lower caste to be treated worse than the animal.

This system is on a Religion basis and has been written in the Hindu religious Books/Granth and Vedas, which is against humanity and full of social discrimination, injustice, inequality and hateful, against the natural law.

Manu Smriti

The Manu Smriti, also known as the Laws of Manu, is an ancient Hindu text that is believed to have been written around 200 BCE. It is considered one of the most important texts in the Hindu tradition and is often cited as a source of guidance on social, moral, and religious issues.

The Manu Smriti is composed of 12 chapters and contains over 2,000 verses. It covers a wide range of topics, including the caste system, marriage, education, inheritance, and the role of women in society. The text also guides religious rituals, such as the performance of sacrifices and the observance of fasts and festivals.

The Manu Smriti has been a controversial text, particularly concerning its treatment of women and the caste system. Some critics argue that it is a reflection of a patriarchal and discriminatory society, while others see it as a source of valuable insights into Hindu culture and tradition. In contemporary times, many Hindus do not consider the Manu Smriti to be binding or authoritative, and there is an ongoing debate about its relevance in modern society.

The Manu Smriti is known for its hierarchical view of society based on the caste system. According to the text, there are four main castes, or varnas, which are ranked in order of social status and spiritual purity. These castes are the Brahmins (priests and scholars), Kshatriyas (warriors and rulers), Vaishyas (merchants and traders), and Shudras (labourers and servants).

The text contains several verses that are critical of the Shudra caste and suggest that they are inferior to the other castes. For example, verse 1.91 states, "the Shudra is born from the feet of Brahmin, Kshatriya and Vaishya; therefore, he should serve them." Several discriminatory rules and practices are based on caste in the Manu Smriti. For example, it prescribes different punishments for the same crime depending on the caste of the offender, and it prohibits intermarriage between castes.

Ramchritmanas

Ramcharitmanas is an epic poem in the Awadhi language, based on the Ramayana, and composed by the 16th-century Indian bhakti poet Tulsidas. In popular parlance, this work is also called Tulsi Ramayana, Tulsikrit Ramayana, Tulsidas Ramayana or simply Manas.

In Ramcharitmanas, there are instances where the social hierarchy of ancient India is mentioned, which places the Brahmins at the top, followed by Kshatriyas, Vaishyas, and Shudras at the bottom. However, many scholars and activists have criticised its hierarchical and discriminatory views. In contemporary times, many Hindus reject the caste system and discrimination.

'Dhol Ganwar Shudra Pashu Nari
Sakal Taadana Ke Adhikari'

Mean: Drum, jungle, Shudra, animal, and woman all deserve punishment.

These contents are controversial and not-acceptable in society.

Unfortunately, discrimination against Shudras (also known as Dalits) and other lower castes is still prevalent in India today, despite constitutional protections and affirmative action policies to promote social equality. Casteism, which refers to the social stratification of people based on their birth into a particular caste, is deeply ingrained in Indian society and continues to influence people's social and economic status and access to education, employment, and other opportunities.

Dalits and other lower castes often face discrimination, harassment, and violence at the hands of members of higher castes, and they continue to struggle for equal treatment and opportunities. While progress has been made in some areas, such as the increase in the representation of Dalits in government and other institutions, there is still a long way to go to eliminate caste-based discrimination and achieve true social equality in India.

Disadvantages & Demerits of the Caste System

Out of Caste System called Ashoot / Untouchable cleaners

1. Undemocratic:- Not working according to democratic principle. No equal rights for all people. The caste system denied equal opportunity for advancement to persons belonging to different castes. It is, therefore, called undemocratic.

2. No Vertical Mobility:- The caste system expected every individual to adopt the occupation prescribed for his caste, which is purely hereditary. Any amount of struggle could not change cast status. Therefore, there was no upward or downward mobility of labour.

3. Encouraged Untouchability:- The Caste system prohibited any physical Contact or communication between Brahmin and Shudra/Ashoot (Untouchable). Even if a Shudra was sighted by a Brahmin at a certain house it was consider polluted. Shadow of Shudra failing on Brahmin would defile him. This it encourages untouchability.

4. Created a Class of Idlers:- Brahmins who were well entrenched at the top of the social hierarchy stopped devoting themselves to study and teaching and started living on alms provided by other castes.

Thus they become parasites of society.

5. Oppression of Low-Caste People:- Restrictions were imposed on low-caste people regarding their place of living, their movements and other activities by high-caste people so that the former may not defile the latter. This resulted in low-caste people being huddled together in a limited area having no access to community and facilities leading a miserable life. Brahmins became virtually tyrants.

6. Encouraged Conversion:- The caste system was solely responsible for the large conversion of people to Christianity and even Islam to an extent. Low-caste people who had no hope of any honourable life had found that by conversion to Islam/Christianity, they could lead a respectable life.

7. Against Integrity of Nation:- The caste system made people more faithful and devoted to their caste than to their nation. Thus caste system made national unity and integrity a difficult task.

8. False Sense of Superiority and Inferiority:- In the caste system, Brahmin was a superior being, simply because he was born as a Brahmin. This was not necessarily matched by his intellectual development and wisdom. On the contrary, anyone born in a low caste was inferior. Members of the high caste considered themselves sole possessors of intellect and wisdom and expected the lower castes to seek their advice before doing anything. This created bad feelings between castes.

9. Nation Not Benefited:- The affairs of the nation were run by a few high-caste people. Thus the nation was deprived of the benefit of the wisdom of the masses.

10. Encouraged Terrorism:- Continuous oppression of low caste people by high caste ones made some of them rebels in society.

*****

Chapter - 12

Combat casteism

Jaat Jaat Mai Jaat Hai Jeo Kellan Ke Paat |

Ravidass Na Manush Jur Sake Jo Lo Jaat Na Jaat || (128)||

(Satguru Ravidass Ji)

Means: Castes have hidden in each caste like the leaf of a banana plant. This caste system cannot be eradicated till all people start living amicably after renouncing their manufactured caste.

Satguru Ravidass Ji has said in his Hymn as stated above that no one loves a slave man we should know that **slavery is a "Sin",** and this system is on a Religion basis and has been written in the Hindu religious Books/ Granth and Vedas which is against humanity and full of social discrimination, injustice, inequality and hateful, against the natural law and that is the reason the Brahminical system has become more corrupted in every field. They spread superstitious & false stories to mislead the person. They have done the work against Nature (God) for a long period and still have the same mindset up and a bug of casteism in their mind has not died. They believe and have faith in the same old mythical literature, and now the present generation has come to know their mind setup. Moreover, Now they are not so powerful and became weak due to their work against humanity and many other reasons.

This time, they are on the extreme (top) now, and it is the law of nature that everything has its limits and all things /goods are perishable. Men also have their limits and are not immortal. Therefore, everybody/everything has to die or will be finished after its time.

How to fight with casteism?

- Every peace-minded person should raise their voice against casteism and destroy all weapons, Atom Bombs, and Dirty

Bombs that can destroy our earth and its creatures. Dirty mind heads of the state or who is controlling our mind can destroy and kill the children before they do, We should do something to stop them and save the future.

- Read & condemn the Books written against community/ humanity. These books/Granth are the guidebooks for the Brahmins system. Change the Scenario; for centuries, Shudras and Ashoots have been treated as animals and still hurt the sentiments and faith of the majority. A bug of casteism is present in the brain of upper caste society.

- Write or consider the Brahmin word in place of Shudra/Ashoot and Shudra in place of Brahmin in the Manu Smriti/ Ramchritmanas. It will be a total change. Oppositely read Manu smriti, i.e. called Tit for Tat. As they did with the literature of aboriginal Indians. Write new Smrities/books, use the Digital way and the same method/weapon. Upper caste people should analyze, who wants to keep their supremacy.

- Promotion of Economic Equality: Very wide economic gap is found between the upper caste and lower caste people. It widens the social distance and contributes to the development of casteism. Hence, all castes should be given equal economic opportunities to attain economic prosperity. The Sense of Caste Prestige is the most important cause of casteism. The feeling of superiority and the Hindu Society is divided in many Castes and that is the reason for weakened the majority of Indians.

- We must bring a nationwide social security system and an education system which will transmit skills to every one according to their aptitude. When this happens, the relevance of the caste system will completely disappear and the caste system will die a natural death.

Follow the method of the system which should be **Horizontal, not vertical** as:

Vertical System

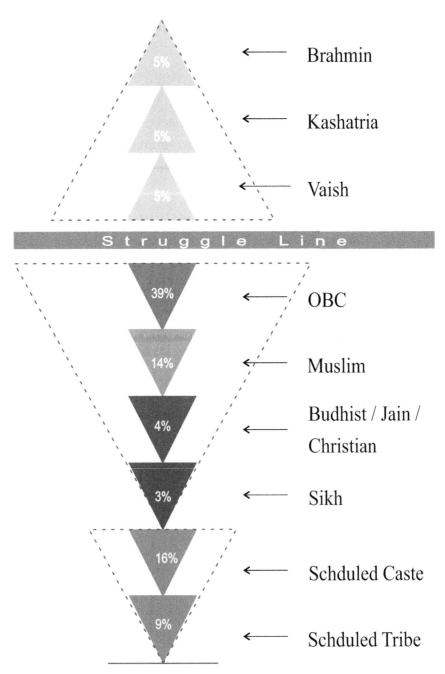

5%	← Brahmin
5%	← Kashatria
5%	← Vaish

S t r u g g l e   L i n e

39%	← OBC
14%	← Muslim
4%	← Budhist / Jain / Christian
3%	← Sikh
16%	← Schduled Caste
9%	← Schduled Tribe

All divided into more than 3000 castes
This system should be breakup

Horizontal System

(Brahmin/Kshatriya/Vaish /OBC/Muslim /Sikh/ SC/ST)

We the people of India i.e. called Bhartiya

Need to be all Equal

To Scheduled Caste, Scheduled Tribes, Other Backward Classes, Buddhists, Jain, Ravidassia, Sikh, Brahmin, Kshatriya, Vaish, Muslim, Christian, etc.

Is it similar to the social hierarchy in Europe, namely royals, nobles and aristocracy, peasants and serfs? Yes, but they do not hate each other but in the caste system, there have hate that does not allow them to come forward.

Remember the **Mool Mantras** of Satguru Ravidass Maharaj ji, Bawa Saheb B.R. Ambedkar, and Babu Kanshi Ram Ji, i.e.

Sat Vidya - Magad Makhira - Pradinta Paap hai
Educate - Organise - Agitate
Light - Fight - Win

Education is a basic need of Humanity. It enlightens our minds and awareness about our surroundings, develops reasoning and light-fights- wins, and if not wins at least save yourselves and your generations. Therefore we should educate our new generations about all the sources of power as discussed above, as well as become Mental & Physically strong, We should become Aristocrats, Scientists, Politician, businessmen, Journalist. Governor, General of the Army, Judge of Apex Court, Commission, Head of the Government's Agencies and there are so many fields in the Govt. Departments.

That's why Satguru Ravidass Ji has given a new concept about the welfare State as stated above that a State/ country should be full of all sources and without any discrimination, living with love and fraternity, and with equality.

**Ravidass Mannukh Kar Basan Kun Sukh Kar Hai Duyi Thav|
Eik Sukh Hai Sav-Raj Mah Dusar Marghat Gavan ||(173)||**

(Satguru Ravidass Ji)

Means: There are two places in the world where a man can live peacefully & happily one is the independent and sovereign state where he can enjoy autonomy. The second is the cremation ground (graveyard), where will sleep forever in a peaceful place.

It is clear that we should capture the power and become the ruler (Be a King of the Kingdom or Die) means do or die for "Power".

"Win in your mind and you will win in your reality".

- For become the ruler of the country, there should be a revolutionary change in the people's political, economic and social life.

- Select one or more places for head office and which will become the Center of Power.

- One Guru/ priest a religious leader who gethered the public then makes a political party, selects a political leader then elect a Ruler of the Country/State.

- Supports Political Party, and for winning, a leader should do everything, the second command should be ready for defeating the ruler and capturing power.

- control should be over administration, money, media, mafia and all of the agencies, and these changes can be in two ways.

Violence & Non-Violence

I. **Violence**

Means Destruction, while the Roman General Vegetius remarked; **Si vis pacem, para bellum** is a Latin adage translated as, **"If you want peace, prepare for war"** (usually interpreted as peace through strength—a strong society less likely to be attacked by enemies).

The Chinese General Sun Tzu advised, "In peace prepare for war, in war prepare for peace";

Aristotle noted, "We make war that we may live in peace"; "If you want peace, prepare for war.

US President Theodore Roosevelt when he coined the phrase **"speak softly, but carry a big stick".** One who "hopes that if he feeds a crocodile, the crocodile will eat him last".

II. Non-violence

The opposite meaning of violence is non-violence, a peaceful method.

"Peace cannot be kept by force; it can only be achieved by understanding." ---- Albert Einstein

Non-violence is peacefully capturing power like in democracy i.e. voting system or organizing the public and peaceful protest against the Government/Ruler for non-cooperation, and the Government compel to surrender, or Ruler will step down due to becoming in the minority. It is a fact that in India, there are living so many kinds of people having different religious faith, and it is clear that nobody alone can get or capture Social, Economic and Political Power unless the people have joined with other like-minded people that's why Satguru Ravidass Ji, Satguru Kabir Ji, Satguru Nanak Ji, Baba Shahab B.R. Ambedkar Ji and Shri Kanshi Ram Ji told us that we should organize a Bahujan Samaj, mean all others who are also suffering from the act and conduct of the Upper Cast or capitalist and having the same thought as Satguru Ravidass Ji said.

Keh Ravidass Khalash Chamara |
Jo Ham Sehri So Meet Hamar ||
(Satguru Ravidass Ji) **Shabad(3)||**

It means that Ravidass, who is pure *Chamar* (doing the work of tanning and making garments and shoes from animal skin), says those who share the same views are our friends.

"It means we should follow the Non-Violence method"

We do not feel an inferiority complex for being a Chamar. Chamar is a holy word written in the Holi Guru Granth Sahab Ji many times by the Guru Arjan Dev Ji, So we are proud to be a Chamar and also called Ravidassia.

When India, i.e. Bharat was called Golden Era, that period was the regime of Ashoka the Great. Ancient India from 3000 BC is the period when India was known as the Golden Sparrow. This era witnessed many famous dynasties like Maurya etc. This era saw cultural confluences and economic booms at many junctures, yet the fabric of traditions never got destroyed. Even today, people sing, 'Jaha Daal Daal Par Sone Ki Chidiya Karti Hai Basera' (where the golden sparrow dwells on every tree branch). Knowledge was considered wealth, and universities like Nalanda and Taxila were renowned worldwide.

Promoting education:- Education is a powerful tool to challenge traditional beliefs and create social awareness. Educating people about the harmful effects of casteism and the importance of social equality can help break down the caste system.

Enforcing laws:- The Indian Constitution prohibits discrimination based on caste, and there are laws in place to protect the rights of lower castes. However, the enforcement of these laws needs to be strengthened to ensure that perpetrators of caste-based discrimination are held accountable.

Raising awareness:- Media, civil society organizations, and other groups can play a vital role in raising awareness about the effects of casteism and promoting social equality. This can include awareness campaigns, advocacy, and social media campaigns.

Promoting inter-caste marriages:- Inter-caste marriages can help break down the caste system and promote social harmony. Promoting and supporting inter-caste marriages and unions can effectively challenge traditional beliefs and promote social equality.

Creating economic opportunities:- Providing economic opportunities to people from lower castes can help break down caste-based discrimination. Providing access to education, training, and employment opportunities can help bridge the gap between different castes and promote social equality.

India's Hindu caste system is a social evil in the society and is condemnable. Various sources translate it into English as a caste or as a social class. Still, the Varna system in Dharma-shastras divides society into four varnas (**Brahmins (priests), Kshatriyas (warriors), Vaishyas (skilled traders, merchants), and Shudras (unskilled workers).** **Shudra** is one of the four varnas. Those who fall out of this system are ostracised as outcastes, called **untouchables/Ashoot** and considered outside the varna system. The people of upper caste, treat the Dalits as in slaved people. These untouchable/Ashoot communities are called in modern times Scheduled Caste and Scheduled Tribes.

Mahatma Jyotirao Govindrao Phule Ji
(11 April1827-28 November 1890)

Views on religion and caste

Phule recast the prevailing Aryan invasion theory of history, proposing that the Aryan conquerors of India, whom the theory's proponents considered to be racially superior, were in fact barbaric suppressors of the indigenous people. He believed that they had instituted the caste system as a framework for subjugation and social division that ensured the pre-eminence of their Brahmin successors.

He saw no change in the subsequent Muslim conquests of the Indian subcontinent as more of the same sort of thing, being a repressive alien regime. But he took heart in the arrival of the British, whom he considered relatively enlightened and not supportive of the varnashrama dharma system instigated and then perpetuated by those previous invaders. In his book, Gulamgiri, he thanked Christian missionaries and the British colonists for making the lower castes realise they were worthy of all human rights. The book, whose title transliterates as slavery and concerned women, caste and reform, was dedicated to the US people working to end slavery.

Phule saw Rama, the hero of the Indian epic Ramayana, as a symbol of oppression stemming from the Aryan conquest. His critique of the caste system began with an attack on the Vedas, the most fundamental texts of upper-caste Hindus. He considered them to be a form of false consciousness.

He is credited with introducing the Marathi word Dalit (broken, crushed) as a descriptor for those people who were outside the traditional varna system. The terminology was later popularised in the 1970s by the Dalit Panthers.

At an education commission hearing in 1884, Phule called for help in providing education for lower castes. To implement it, he advocated making primary education compulsory in villages. He also asked for special incentives to get more lower-caste people into high schools and colleges.

Sathyashodhak Samaj On 24 September 1873, Phule formed Satyashodhak Samaj to focus on the rights of depressed groups such as women, the Shudra, and the Dalit. Through this organisation, he opposed idolatry and denounced the caste system. Satyashodhak Samaj campaigned for the spread of rational thinking and rejected the need for priests.

Phule established Satyashodhak Samaj with the ideals of human well-being, happiness, unity, equality, and easy religious principles and rituals. A Pune-based newspaper, Deenbandhu, provided the voice for the views of the Samaj.

The members of the samaj included Muslims, Brahmans, and government officials. However,non-Brahman castes dominated. Phule's own Mali caste provided the leading members and financial supporters for the organization.

Occupation: Apart from his **role as a social activist, Phule** was a businessman too. He established has business supplying metal-casting equipment in 1863.

1.   **Phule** is credited with introducing the Marathi word **Dalit (meaning broken, crushed)** to describe those outside the varna system. In the 1970s, the term was made popular by the Dalit Panthers.

2.   **Phule** inspired BR Ambedkar, India's first law minister and architect of our Constitution. Ambedkar not only acknowledged **Phule** as one of his three gurus but also drew inspiration from him.

3.   In 1884, at a hearing of the education commission, **Phule demanded compulsory primary education** in villages and incentives for the socially underprivileged in schools and colleges.

4.   After many years of marriage, when **Jyoti Rao Phule and** Savitribai did not have children. In 1873, the couple adopted the son of a widow who came to their infanticide prevention centre for delivery.

5.   He started the **Satyashodhak marriage system** which involved marriage rituals and alternative verses that contained egalitarian content. The Bombay HC later recognised this system.

Shahu Chhatrapati Ji
Date of Birth:-26-06-1874

Legacy: Social and Educational Reforms, Opposed Brahman Supremacy.

Chhatrapati Shahu Maharaj, also known as Rajarshi Shahu, was considered a true democrat and social reformer. First Maharaja of the princely state of Kolhapur, he was an invaluable gem in the history of Maharashtra. Greatly influenced by the contributions of social reformer Jyotiba Phule, Shahu Maharaj was an ideal leader and able ruler who was associated with many progressive and path-breaking activities during his rule. He worked tirelessly for the cause of the lower caste subjects in his state. Primary education to all, regardless of caste and creed, was one of his most important priorities.

Social Reforms:- Chhatrapati Shahu occupied the throne of Kolhapur for 28 years, from 1894 to 1922, and during this period, he initiated numerous social reforms in his empire. His emphasis was on education, and he aimed to make education available to the masses. He introduced several educational programs to promote education among his subjects. He established hostels separately for different ethnicities and religions like Panchals, Devadnya, Nabhik, Shimpi, and Dhor-Chambhar communities and as well as for Muslims, Jains and Christians. He established the Miss Clarke Boarding School for the socially quarantined segments of society. He introduced several scholarships for poor but deserving students from backward castes. He also initiated a compulsory free primary education for all in his state. He established Vedic Schools that enabled students from all castes and classes to learn the scriptures and propagate Sanskrit education among all. He also started special schools for the village heads or 'Patils' to make them into better administrators.

Chhatrapati Sahu strongly advocated equality among all strata of society and refused to give the Brahmins any special status. He removed Brahmins from the post of Royal Religious advisers when they refused to perform religious rites for non-Brahmins. He appointed a young Maratha scholar in the post and bestowed him the title of `Kshatra Jagadguru' (the world teacher of the Kshatriyas). This incident and the Shahu's encouragement of the non-Brahmins to read and recite the Vedas led to the Vedokta controversy in Maharashtra. The Vedokta controversy brought a storm of protest from the elite strata of the society, a vicious opposition to the Chhatrapati's rule. He established the Deccan Rayat Association in Nipani in 1916. The association sought to secure political rights for non-Brahmins and invite their equal participation in politics. The works of Jyotirao Phule influenced Shahuji, and he long patronized the Satya Shodhak Samaj, formed by Phule. In his later life, he, however, moved towards the Arya Samaj.

Chhatrapati Shahu made great efforts to abolish the concept of caste segregation and untouchability. He introduced (perhaps the first

95

known) reservation system in government jobs for untouchable castes. His Royal Decree ordered his subjects to treat every member of society as equal. He granted the untouchables equal access to public utilities like wells and ponds and establishments like schools and hospitals. He legalised inter-caste marriages and made a lot of efforts for the upliftment of the Dalits. He discontinued the hereditary transfer of titles and tenures of revenue collectors (Kulkarni), a caste infamous for exploiting the masses, especially the enslavement of the lower caste Mahars.

The Chhatrapati also worked towards the betterment of the conditions of women in his empire. He established schools to educate women and also spoke vociferously on the topic of women's education. He introduced a law banning the Devadasi Pratha, the practice of offering girls to God, which essentially led to the exploitation of the girls in the hands of the Clergy. He legalised widow remarriages in 1917 and made efforts towards stopping child marriages.

He introduced several projects that enabled his subjects to self-sustain in their chosen professions. The Shahu Chhatrapati Spinning and Weaving Mill, dedicated marketplaces, and establishment of co-operative societies for farmers were introduced by the Chhatrapati to alleviate his subjects from middle men in trading. He made credits available to farmers looking to buy equipment to modernise agricultural practices and even established the King Edward Agricultural Institute to teach farmers to increase crop yield and related technologies. He initiated the Radhanagari Dam on February 18, 1907, and the project was completed in 1935. The dam stands testament to Chhatrapati Shahu's vision towards the welfare of his subjects and made Kolhapur self-sufficient in water.

He was a great patron of art and culture and encouraged artists from music and fine arts. He supported writers and researchers in their endeavours. He installed gymnasiums and wrestling pitches and highlighted the importance of health consciousness among the youth.

His seminal contribution to social, political, educational,

agricultural and cultural spheres earned him the title of Rajarshi, which was bestowed upon him by the Kurmi warrior community of Kanpur.

Association with Dr B. R. Ambedkar

Chhatrapati was introduced to Bhimrao Ambedkar by artists Dattoba Pawar and Dittoba Dalvi. The King was greatly impressed by the great intellect of young Bhimrao and his revolutionary ideas regarding untouchability. The two met several times during 1917-1921 and went over possible ways to abolish the negatives of caste segregation. Together they organised a conference for the betterment of the untouchables during March 21-22, 1920 and Chhatrapati made Dr Ambedkar the Chairman as he believed that Dr Ambedkar was the leader who would work for the amelioration of the segregated segments of the society. He even donated Rs. 2,500 to Dr Ambedkar when he started his newspaper 'Mooknayak' on January 31, 1921, and contributed more later for the same cause. Their association lasted till Chhartapati's death in 1922.

Erode Venkata Ramasamy Periyar
1879-1973 Tamil Nadu,

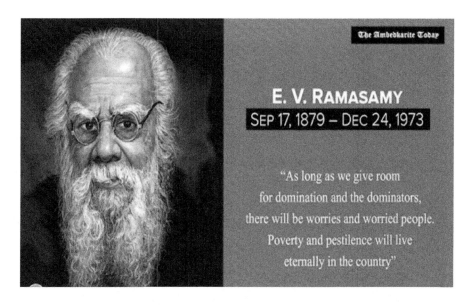

Self-Respect Movement, Dravidian Nationalism, against

97

Brahminical dominance, caste prevalence and **women oppression** in Tamilnadu.

He opposed the exploitation and marginalisation of the **non-Brahmin Dravidian** people of South India and the imposition of what he considered **Indo-Aryan** India.Early years

Ambedkar with Ramaswami Periyar

At a young age, he began questioning the apparent contradictions in **Hindu mythological stories**. As Periyar grew, he felt that people used religion only as a mask to deceive innocent people and therefore took it as one of his duties in life to warn people against superstitions and priests.

Who was Erode Venkata Ramasamy Periyar?

Erode Venkata Ramasamy Periyar was born in 1879 in what was then called the Madras Presidency to a Kannada businessman and later joined his father's business. He joined the Congress party but left it after he found it to be dominated by the Brahmins. Much later, he started his own Dravidar Kazhagam party, which is considered the inspiration of all political parties and launched later on the plank of Tamil pride.

What was E.V Ramasamy Periyar politics?

Periyar's thoughts, philosophy and actions revolved around his opposition to Brahminism. He said Brahmins had dominated all other castes through their religious principles and practices. He propounded rationalism and criticised the Hindu religion as superstitious.

However, he believed in the ideas of Tamil saint Thiruvalluvar and hence held faith in the idea of a single, formless God. He found conversion to Islam and Christianity as a way for the lower castes to escape Brahmin oppression, as he thought both these religions created better societies than Hinduism. Periyar was also against Mahatma Gandhi because he saw Gandhi as not rejecting Brahminical ideas and practices.

Periyar's Self-respect movements

Periyar became known widely as a leader of the lower castes after he led a movement in 1924 that demanded the entry of Dalits into temples in Kerala. However, he is known the most for his Self-respect Movement that aimed at generating pride in lower castes.

His campaign against the imposition of Hindi in Tamil Nadu is the origin of all anti-Hindi movements later in south India. He found Hindi a tool of the Brahminical domination of the Tamils. His most controversial movement was protesting against Hindu idols. The movement involved breaking or burning of idols of Hindu gods or garlanding them with shoes.

Why is Periyar such a big issue today?

Even though many Dalits find Periyar to be a representative of non-Brahmin upper castes, he has been a big anti-caste icon in India. His importance is more important due to his centrality to the Tamil pride movement.

Today, no political party can hope to succeed in Tamil Nadu politics if it does not swear by Periyar. So even the BJP, which can hope to achieve little in Tamil Nadu politics alone, cannot afford to be seen opposing Periyar. Perhaps that's by BJP leader Raja regretted his Facebook post against Periyar.

Top Quotes of Periyar

There is no god, there is no god, and there is no god at all.

He who invented god is a fool.

He who propagates god is a scoundrel.

He who worships god is a barbarian.

Man is equal to man. There should not be exploitation. One should help the other. No one should harm anybody. Generally, there should be no room for grievance or complaint from anybody. Everyone should live and let others live, with a national spirit.

Man treats woman as his own property and not as being capable of feelings, like himself. The way a man treats women is much worse than the way landlords treat servants and the high-caste treat the low-caste. They treat them so demeaningly only in situations mutually affecting them, but men treat them cruelly and as slaves, from their birth to death. Brahmins, before all of us by promising, to ensure the supply of rice & cereals to our fore-father through their false mantras & rituals. Is it a wise deed?

By helping the poor, we must be able to remove their poverty. But extending help to one here and one there in the form of providing food will not remove poverty.

I want the Brahmins to realize that the Dravidian people today are very much hating those who cunningly cheated them with absurdities. They are now aware of the particular community making a living by spreading foolishness. People have begun to hate god, religion, caste, mythologies (Puranas) and so on

While all men are born as equals, to say that Brahmins alone are the highest and all others are low as Pariah (the Untouchables) or Panchama is sheer non-sense. It is roguish to say so. It is a big hoax played on us.

The number of those who do selfless public service and those who serve without expecting any return should increase. Their sterling qualities should show the way to the people at large. Their life would be a model to show how a man should conduct himself in public life.

Because our ladies mostly attend Kalatshepams (Religious discourses), they have fallen prey to the superstitions, blind beliefs, and immorality by the false and fictitious propaganda of the Brahmins.

A male has the right to wander about as he pleases. He has the right to marry any number of girls. This practice has led to prostitution.

Capitalists control the machinery. They create difficulties for the workers. Consequently, rationalism, which has to lead the way for peaceful life for all, has resulted in causing poverty and worries to the people because of dominating forces.

Those who still believe the Brahmins should take serious note of the changing times and start leading an awakened life.

Modern Slavery is all around us but often just out of sight.

"The biggest enemy you have to deal with is yourself.
If there's no enemy within, then the enemy outside can do us no
harm." ~ Les Brown.

Story of Baby Elephant:-

These limitations inevitably lead to many of us suffering from the "**Baby Elephant syndrome.**" The story is told about how elephants are trained. When an elephant lives in captivity and is still a baby, it is tied to a tree with a chain or rope nightly. The baby elephant tries with all its might to break the rope but it isn't strong enough to do so. It tries and fails many times until realizing its efforts are futile, it finally gives up and stops attempting for the rest of its life.

Later, when the elephant is fully grown, it can be tied to a small tree with a thin rope and could easily free itself by breaking the rope or uprooting the tree but because its mind has been conditioned by its past experiences, it doesn't even make the slightest attempt to break free. This powerful animal has confined its present abilities by the limitations of past experiences hence, the "Baby Elephant Syndrome.

Human beings are similar to the elephant except for one thing, we can choose not to accept the false boundaries created by others or the past.

As per the above-said examples, we all know the life of an enslaved person. He has no life, wish, land, or home; moreover, he can not do anything without the permission of his master`s order, and he bears suffering, cruelty, and maltreatment at the hands of his master/ owner.

So Satguru Ravidass Ji said it is a **Sin.** Sin means wrongdoers, wrongful acts and things unacceptable in Society, against Humanity and Law. Therefore, it means one should not be enslaved. Do not become slave it is a Sin.

> *" The mind is a powerful force. It can enslave us or empower us. It can plunge us into the depths of misery or take us to the heights of ecstasy. Learn to use is wisely."*
>
> *~David Cuschieri*

To keep up the mind of a person, Satguru Ravidass Ji said,

"Man Changa Kathoti main Ganga"

Assuming good Ganga in Kathoti (Pot)

The Seven tips to break the chains that are holding you captive.

1. Believe in yourself:- You have to believe in yourself ultimately. Always Think big and Dream big. Focus on your strengths and work on developing your shortfalls. Don't compare yourself to others and don't let circumstances dictate what you are capable of achieving.

"Believe in yourself and there will come a day when others will

have no choice but to believe with you." Cynthia Kersey

2. Work hard:- Do what you can do. Don't waste time feeling sorry for yourself. Take responsibility for where you are. Stop feeling like you're owed. In life, there are no handouts. If you want something, you owe it to yourself to go out and get it. Nothing worth having comes easy.

> *"Determination and perseverance move the world;thinking that others will do it for you is a sure way to fail."*
> *~Marva Collins*

3. Be Positive:- *Turn* **negatives into positives** and make it a growing experience. Don't dwell on others' opinions of you or take things personally. Don't blame and harbour toxic emotions. It will only hold you back. Let it add fuel to the fire.

Envision the future and maintain your focus.

> *"As I walked out the door toward the gate that would lead to my freedom. I knew if I didn't leave my bitterness and hatred behind, I'd still be in prison." ~Nelson Mandela*

4. Never give up:- Be confident. Ask for what you want. Purpose in your heart that you will keep fighting for your dreams. How many times will you try before you decide to give up? This is your dream and you have to protect it. I try every door until I have exhausted all options and yet I don't give up. Once there is a will, there is always way and I am determined to find it!

> *"You've only got three choices in life :*
> *Give up, give in, or give it all you've got.*

5. Be Patient:- For everything, there is a time and season. The waiting period can be the most difficult but it's important to not let doubt and fear creep in.

> *"No matter how great the talent or efforts, some things just take time. "You can't produce a baby in one month by getting nine women pregnant"*

103

6. Have a strong support network:- You can't do it alone. There are days when it becomes too much for you. You may need a little help to get back up.

"Surround yourself with **the dreamers and the doers, the believers and thinkers, but most of all,** *surround yourself with* **those who** *see the greatness* **within you."** ~Edmund Lee

7. Have faith: that things will work out. Some things are out of your control. I trust that God will take me through those difficult moments and this gives me peace even when things don't go my way.

"Faith is like the *radar* **that sees through the fog"**

~Corrie Ten Boom.

Additionally, as my grandmother would always say, **"Make books your friends!"** It opens your mind to new possibilities and helps you learn from the experience of others.

The saddest state a person can reach is mental slavery. They have already given up. Every day I counsel individuals and I wish I could make them believe in themselves, but I can't. They will have to remove the shackles for themselves. This is your life!

"Don't let anyone else write your story. Take back the pen and make a great ending!

"None can destroy iron but its own *rust* **can. Likewise, none can destroy a person, but his own mindset can"**
~*Ratan Tata*.

Self-defence

- Be careful in future from the non-humanitarian/Brahmin they first will create fear and then give greediness, and false promises, creating Jumla (bogus) and then they will snatch your liberty.

- So, creating an Organisation may be religious or political, agitate / revolt against the cruel ruler and compel them to leave the kingdom or Regine or put him down.

- To make management committees, who will arrange and provide the Food, make Shelter, Health care centre, Teaching and coaching centre, Clothes, Transportation, and contain human amenities.

- To maintain the proper discipline and make rules and regulations.

- To become the Land Lord, Capture the natural resources one by one and institutions.

- To become resourceful/powerful and rich in every field.

- Opening of Training Center for Self-defence, Institution of Education & Coaching center.

So, the above-said examples and quotations regarding slavery and how to come out of slavery are critical points to learn for a person who is depressed and belongs to a low caste. It is psychotherapy and motivation for the person to make his mind powerful, and nobody should think low or below others. Develop your mind through education and information. It is very important & essential to acquire all-around knowledge to be a great person. The brain of a human being is very much powerful. If you know the brain, you can know the Universe. Every great person has more knowledge and information. Once a person has the education, he will be aware of his right and has to fight against discrimination. After that, he can be a leader to lead the society to become the Ruler of the country.

*****

Part -3

Chapter -13

By becoming the Ruler

Before you know how to become the Ruler of the State or Country. You must know what is a **state** and how to run it successfully. Learn about state:

Concept of State

Now the question is, what is a state and the concept of the welfare state? And how we can make the welfare State which the Saint/Guru and leader has told us to go ahead with, i.e. the master key of Political Power. What is Political Power and the concept of State? A state can be with or without religion, but the majority of the population has religion and with religion, a community can organise and learn many things.

Aisa Chahu Raj Main Jahan Milai Sabhan Ko Aun|

Chot-barrai Sabh Sum Basai Ravidass Rahai Parsan||

(Satguru Ravidass Ji) **SALOK || 174 ||**

This **mean**s:- I want such a regime where everybody gets sufficient food and enjoys equal rights. No one dies of hunger. Ravidass will be happy to see such a country where there is no discrimination between the lower and upper classes.

Now, it is very important to know about the state and what is the welfare State and its meaning.

The meaning & theory of the State

A **state** is an organized **political** community acting under a government. **States** may be classified as sovereign if they are not dependent on, or "**State** is a combination or association of persons in the form of government and governed and sovereign united together on the part of Land.

106

The state has four essential elements
1. Land.
2. Population.
3. Government.
4. Sovereignty,

All the above elements are essential for a State; without any of these elements, a State can not be recognised as a State.

As per the other theory of the State, it also matched the above-said element:-

1. King.
2. Minister,
3. Capital,
4. Real (Area overseen by a King),
5. Treasury,
6. Army,
7. Ally (Unity/Organisation).

All elements revolve around two elements i.e. King and Kingdom, as described below:-

King and Kingdom:- A politically organized community or major territorial unit has a monarchical form of government headed by a king or queen.

King is the head of the State who controls and enjoys all the power of the Kingdom or state. How the King uses his power depends on the nature of the King. It might be soft-hearted or hard-hearted means democratize or dictatorship means if the King takes the decision in favour of the citizen and do the development for the welfare of the State as desires of its citizen, then the King called democratically and if the King takes the decision as per his own wish and against the public then the King called a dictator. A Dictator always becomes cruel and misuses his power to suppress the rights of the citizens.

Many Kings came to India, established their kingdoms, and ruled the country as per their religion and culture. The other King challenged them, fought many battles, and many things happened. Knows the brief history of India and the Indian civilisation since the Indus Valley.

Based on religion, who becomes the emperor is as below:

Indian civilisation (Indus Valley)

1. Aryans/Brahmanism- became Emperor in 2000 to 1500 BCE

2. Ashoka/Buddhist   became Emperor in 261 BCE

3. Muslim became Emperor in 1206 AD

4. Sikh became Emperor in 1799 AD

5. Christian became Emperor in India in 18th century

Islam came onto the scene and spread rapidly only after it began to use the SWORD...conquer...and take over political power...the Caliphates. The Mughal Empire. Today Islam is the power behind the Governments of more than 50; remove that power and bring democracy. Freedom of religion. And Islam will rapidly decline.

Christianity began its rapid spread once the KINGS were converted....thus Europe turned Christian soon after...then came the Christian Roman Empire...Crusades. etc.

Christianity spread worldwide due to the " Christian Whiteman" grabbing political power and Colonising the world.

RELIGION cannot spread rapidly without Political Power; Political Power; is essential to speed up the rapid spread of a "religion....or any other ideology".

IF Religion/Dharam has neglected, Then **ABSOLUTE POWER will be CORRUPTED ABSOLUTELY**, as is happening worldwide in many countries and so-called Religious Countries. It is also true for political ideologies like Communism and Marxism; These would have remained theories on paper. If not successfully grabbing and keeping a stranglehold on political power in USSR Eastern Europe, China,

Vietnamese etc. When this power was absolute and in the hands of a few. It fell as in the fall of the USSR. Eastern Europe and maybe slowly happening in China. Suppose these Leaders had some "goodness" like Dharam backing their actions. They would have succeeded a little longer. But they became dictators, Stalin, Lenin, and Khrushchev, with no morality of good actions.

All become emperors based on their power, strength, planning and the philosophy of the religion.

Now it is your turn, So be ready but think positively and minutely that nobody will give the empire on a plate. There will be a struggle. Look at history every time the present ruler has not allowed the opponent to cross the struggle lane. They will try their best to stop you by hook or crook and apply all the methods they have written in their religious books. The King represents God, and the king can do no wrong.

It means King has all the powers. Now think about this, who and how can be a King? Prepare the road map, make a plan, join like-minded people, near dears, form a big organisation, show the power strength and converted into **Vote or Warrior.**

Along with devotion, strength is also needed. (Power with devotion)

War is won not by becoming martyrs but by making the enemy martyrs.

*****

Chapter - 14

Welfare State

In the modern system, the definition of a welfare state is a system organized by a government to provide free services and money for people who have no job, who are ill, etc. The **concept of government of a State plays a key role in the protection and promotion of the economic and social well-being of citizens.** In detail, Satguru Ravidass Ji has described in the hymn of Begampura Shabad, and it is an obvious definition and meaning of the welfare state. The welfare state also depends on the Ruler as well as on Government. Several different types of governments exist worldwide, each with unique characteristics and structures. Some of the most common forms of government include:

1. Democracy:- A system of government in which power is held by the people, usually through elected representatives. It is based on the principles of political equality, popular sovereignty, and the rule of law. In a democracy, citizens have the right to participate in the political process through voting and other forms of political engagement. They also have the right to express their opinions freely, assemble peacefully, and petition their government to redress grievances.

Democratic governments are characterized by a separation of powers among the branches of government, i.e., the legislative, executive, and judicial branches, and a system of checks and balances to prevent any branch or individual from accumulating too much power.

Overall, democracy is a system of government that values the input and participation of the people and seeks to ensure that power is exercised responsibly and in the best interests of society as a whole.

Democracy is an illusion or meaningless if we are not aware; About Our Rights, About the Right to Vote,

There are some demerits of Democracy; for example, the candidate who receives the highest number of votes in a constituency wins, regardless of whether or not they have an absolute majority (i.e.

more than 50% of the votes). For example where four candidates are running for office in a constituency and the results are as follows:

Candidate A - 15%
Candidate B - 20%
Candidate C - 30%
Candidate D - 35%

In this scenario, Candidate D has received the highest number of votes and would be declared the winner, even though they only have the support of 35% of the voters. This means that 65% of the voters have voted for other candidates, and their preferred candidate has not won.

However, the system remains in place in India for the time being. Even then, Democracy should be saved, and work for its strengthen. Strengthening democratic institutions: Institutions like the judiciary, legislature, and executive need to be strengthened and insulated from political interference. It should be an Independent and impartial institution and which protects free and fair elections.

2. **Monarchy:-** A system of government in which a single person, usually a king or queen, holds supreme power and inherits the position.

3. Dictatorship:- A form of government in which a single person, known as a dictator, holds absolute power and authority, dictatorships are often characterized by oppression, violence, and instability, often short-lived and can be overthrown or removed from power through popular uprisings, coups, or military interventions.

4.Theocracy:- A system of government in which religious leaders hold power and authority over the state.

5. **Communism:-** A political and economic system in which all property and resources are owned and controlled by the state.

6. **Fascism:-** A political ideology that emphasizes strong centralized government, nationalism, and authoritarianism.

7.Anarchy:- A system in which there is no formal government or authority.

These are just a few examples of the various government forms, and also we have to know how to become the head of the Government or Ruler of the State.

In the last it is observed that the sociolism democracy is a good government as Satguru Ravidass Ji has stated in his hymn, "Begampura", as well as written in the definition of Ravidassia religion i.e;

"Ravidassia Religion preached and based on the Universal Truth, Gospel of Universal Brotherhood, Love and Fraternity, Equality, Humanity, and Casteless Society, based on Logical concepts supported by the public".

*****

Chapter - 15

How to become the Ruler

A ruler is a person who rules or commands the public, and the public obeys the command and thinks for the betterment of society and their's future. Becoming Rulers of the State, we should involve gaining political power and authority through various means. Here are some common ways that someone can become a ruler of a State or country:

1. Monarchy or Inheritance:- One can become a country's ruler by inheriting the throne from a family member who is already a ruler. This is known as a monarchy or a hereditary system of government. A king or queen can be created through marriage or social relations.

2. Election:- In a democratic system, individuals can become rulers of a country by running for office and winning an election. This is often the case in presidential or parliamentary systems of government.

3. Coup:- Sometimes, a person can become a ruler by forcibly overthrowing the existing government in a coup d'etat(unseat). This is an illegal and often violent way to take power.

4. Revolution:- Another way to become a ruler is through a popular revolution, where the people rise up against the existing government and replace it with a new system of government.

5. Appointment:- In some cases, a person can become a ruler by being appointed to the position by an existing ruler or government. This can happen in situations where the country has a strong central authority, and the ruler has the power to appoint officials.

It's important to note that becoming a ruler is a complex process involving political, social, and historical factors. In most cases, becoming a ruler involves a long and challenging journey that requires great skill, determination, and willingness to take risks.

To become a Ruler, first of all, have the command of the people and become the **leader** of the masses, and the public should obey the leader's order. To become a leader, learn about the qualities of a **leader.**

"Win in your mind, and you will win in your reality".

To become a leader

To overcome the fear, become the leader or develop the leadership quality, lead the public, and fight for their rights.

"If you make an army of 100 lions, the commander is a dog, all lions will be killed in war. But if you form an army of 100 dogs whose commander is a lion, all dogs will fight like a lion in war."

#Napoleon_Bonaparte (1769 - 1821)

Be a good leader to change the concept of Society and leads a big group of people. How to be a good leader, as **Sonya Krakoff**, who is the Senior Content Marketing Specialist at Champlain College Online, has written about leadership: Who then is a leader?

Countless people have led people throughout history but were inhumane and destructive. Does that still make them leaders? In my mind, a leader does more than just lead people. They have to be driven by the right motivation and make a positive impact on the people around them.

A leader can see how things can be improved and rallies people to move toward that better vision. Leaders can work toward making their vision a reality while putting people first. Just being able to motivate people isn't enough — leaders need to be empathetic and connect with people to be successful at the grassroots.

Leaders don't have to come from the same background or follow the same path. Future leaders will actually be more diverse, bringing various perspectives. He helps to promote the right people and maintain a cohesive work environment. Everyone knows what leadership is, but few people can actually put it.

The quality of a leader

1. Vision:- Perhaps the greatest quality any leader can have is vision - the ability to see the big picture of where the organization or team they are working within is headed, **what it's capable of, and what it will take to get there.**

2. Inspiration:- Equally as important as having a vision is the ability to convey that vision to others and get them excited about it. It means maintaining a positive yet realistic presence within the organization helping team members stay motivated and engaged.

3. Strategic & Critical Thinking:- A good leader will be able to think critically about the organization or team they work within and develop a clear understanding of its strengths, weaknesses, opportunities, and threats (and how they, as an individual, can work to support or overcome these). They'll be able to course-correct when necessary and assess their work to determine how it fits into overall organizational strategy and goals.

4. Interpersonal Communication:- Good leaders must be able to interact with others in a genuine way. It does not mean you must be an extrovert or a people-person to be a leader - many excellent leaders self-identify as introverts! Rather, it means demonstrating empathy, engaging in active listening, and building meaningful working relationships with those around you, whether they are a peer or direct reports.

5. Authenticity & Self-Awareness:- One of the key ways to become a great leader is to be self-aware enough to understand your strengths and your flaws and to build an authentic leadership style that's true to who you are and how you do your best work. You want to be the best possible leader you can be, not try to fit into a mould set by someone else. Try to embrace the things that make you who you are, which will naturally translate into developing an authentic leadership style.

6. Open-Mindedness & Creativity:- Being a good leader means being open to new ideas, possibilities, and perspectives and understanding that there's no "right" way to do things. Leadership involves the knowledge that success comes with a willingness to change things and bring in fresh eyes to inspire new ideas and try to think outside the box as much as possible. Leaders must be able to listen, observe, and capacity to change the concept of mind of a person.

7. Flexibility:- Leadership also means being adaptable and agile when the situation calls for it. Nothing ever goes according to plan - whether you encounter minor roadblocks or large obstacles, you must be prepared to stop, reassess, and determine a new course of action. Good leaders will embrace the ever-changing nature of business and meet challenges with a flexible attitude - and be able to build and inspire that same willingness to adapt in those around them.

8. Responsibility & Dependability:- One of the most important qualities a leader can have is a sense of responsibility and dependability. It means displaying those traits in your work and demonstrating them in your interactions with others. Your team members need to know they can depend on you to take on your fair share of work and follow through, support them through tough times, and help them meet shared and individual goals.

9. Patience & Tenacity:- A good leader knows how to take the long view, whether it's of a strategy, a situation, or a goal. Being able to take on any bumps in the road and persist on without getting frustrated or defeated is key—from small projects to corporate vision, patience is a trait that is essential to strong leadership.

10. Continuous Improvement:- True leaders know that perfection is a myth. There is always room for improvement on all levels, from the personal to the team to the overall organization. They'll always be willing to help the team member find ways to develop new skills or improve upon a weakness, identify and implement strategies for helping the organization as a whole grow, and, perhaps most importantly, be able to look inward. Identify the areas they would like to work on, then act on them.

How to Become a Great Leader and Develop Leadership Skills

Even the most junior team members **can learn how to be good leaders** if they use their talents to boost, motivate and assist their teams in moving forward and ultimately accomplishing their goals. And more broadly, one can lead in many contexts beyond the workplace, in any community with which you might be involved (for example, a religious community, a volunteer community, or a neighbourhood community). Even if your sphere of influence is relatively small, you can play an integral role in leading the organization to success.

Leadership does not belong to those at the top of the organizational hierarchy, nor does it only apply to people with what we would commonly consider leadership qualities (an outgoing personality, for example). It's also important to note that though we often refer to leadership as a singular skill, it's an accumulation of skills (most of which can be developed through experience and training) uniquely influenced by an individual's personality and background. Think about your adventure: of the leaders you've interacted with throughout your life, several different leadership styles are represented. However, most of them probably possessed similar good leadership qualities that they drew from to be successful.

Leadership is a competency, unlike some highly specialized or technical skills. It can be accessible to anyone, regardless of where they fall on an organizational chart. Similarly, anyone can, whether through formal training or self-education and on-the-job leadership development and its skill and practice. Be a good speaker, speak on the public issues & become a captain of a team.

For example, if you are a relatively junior member of your organization, you might want to look at the qualities of leadership listed above and assess how you do on each of them. Maybe you'll recognize some of them as traits you possess, and perhaps some of them are places you could work on developing. That could mean practising active listening during meetings with co-workers, being proactive about bringing new ideas to your team or asking for assistance from a peer or manager in developing one of your weaker areas.

It is a process. When a person becomes a good leader and leads the masses, power will automatically be in his path. What is the Power we have to learn about power.

Chapter - 16

What is Power?

Power means authority, command, control, dominion, jurisdiction, and sway. While all these words mean "the right to govern or rule or determine," power implies possessing the ability to wield force, authority, or influence. A person that influences other people is a person's power. The ability to act or produce an effect. It's in your power to change things. The right to do something the Ruler's powers. Physical might: Strength. The wind grew in power i.e.

a) Social Power,
b) Economic Power and
c) Political Power

Social Power:- That the social status of an individual by itself often becomes a source of power and authority is made clear by the sway (enjoy), now, the question is why social reform is necessary for economic reform and why social reform is necessary for political reform.

EXAMPLES OF SOCIAL POWER

Social power is an essential element for uplifting Society, as well as **Social Justice**, **Social Equality**, and **Social freedom**, and these are all involved in Social power, which has defined as:-

"**the ability to set standards, create norms and values that are deemed legitimate and desirable, without resorting to coercion or payment**", is a central part of contemporary international politics. Who has social power?

Social power is a form of power that is **found in society and within politics**. While physical power relies upon strength to force another person to act, social power is found within the rules of society and laws of the land. It rarely uses one-on-one conflicts to force others to act in ways they normally would not. **Social roots are a very important element. Organise the intellectual brains, experienced persons and money holders. These are the generators to develop the quality of organisation of Heart and Brain to run the organisation and for making successful Social organisations and for non-political roots.** Educate the Society, organise them and then struggle for freedom, self-respect, rights and equality, i.e. Social, Economical and political. The social status, self-respect and identity of a person are very important.

> **Kahi Ravidass Khalas Chamara |**
> **Jo Ham Sahri So Meet Hamara ||**
> (Satguru Ravidass Ji) **Shabad(3)||**

"No value or status without identity, so be bold."

Economical Power :- Economic power is the ability of countries, businesses, or individuals to improve their standard of living. It increases their freedom to make decisions that benefit themselves alone and reduces the ability of any outside force to reduce their independence. Purchasing power is a significant component of economic power. The economy, such as capitalism, socialism, and communism, works in the real world.

Capture the institutions, open Bank, and get the mines, minerals and natural resources, infrastructure, possession of land, water and air, start your business and control all over the economical platforms for the betterment of the public & our self.

How does the government control the economy?

When it comes to the economy, governments **set economic rules known as regulations, collect taxes, and spend money on infrastructure development and the welfare of the citizens**. But governments can also regulate the economy in more ways behind the scenes. The Government has given equal importance to Agriculture, industries, and trade, forming part of the economy in the Vaarta' science. There was no absolute poverty or unemployment at that time. It is also because right earning also formed part of the wealth.

If we are economically weak, we can not survive better in society, making planning to become financially strong. On the other hand, if you are economically strong, your life status will automatically change. Then you can survive happily with your family, educate the children in a good institute, purchase land, bungalows, and vehicles and help society. Therefore the economy is the most significant factor that made India the golden bird in an earlier period. The gold coins were issued. The currency and numismatics during the period are widely known for their efficiency and perfection.

Political Power:- Politics is the struggle among the people for power. Politics is the way that people living in groups make decisions. Politics is about making agreements between people so that they can live together in groups such as tribes, cities, or countries. Politicians and sometimes others may get together to form a government.

Politics in India:- India is a parliamentary democratic republic in which the president of India is the head of state, and the prime minister of India is the head of government. India follows the dual polity system, i.e. federal in nature, that consists of the central authority at the centre and states at the periphery.

Positional power", legitimate power, is the power of an individual because of the relative position and duties of the holder of the position within an organization. Legitimate power is formal authority delegated to the holder of the position. It is usually accompanied by various attributes of power, such as a uniform, a title, or an imposing physical office.

Thus a political regime maintains power because people accept and obey its dictates, laws and policies. People will also choose different tactics based on the group situation and based on whom they wish to influence. People also tend to shift from soft to hard tactics when they face resistance.

Positive Power:- Power prompts people to take action. Makes individuals more responsive to changes within a group and its environment. They are more proactive, more likely to speak up, make the first move, and lead the negotiation. They are more focused on the goals appropriate in a given situation and tend to plan more task-related activities in a work setting. They tend to experience more positive emotions, such as happiness and satisfaction, and they smile more than low-power individuals. Power is associated with optimism about the future because more powerful individuals focus their attention on more positive aspects of the environment. People with more power tend to carry out executive cognitive functions more rapidly and successfully, including internal control mechanisms that coordinate attention, decision-making, planning, and goal selection.

Negative Power:- Powerful people are prone to take risky, inappropriate, or unethical decisions and often overstep their boundaries. They tend to generate negative emotional reactions in their subordinates, particularly when there is a conflict in the group. When individuals gain power, their self-evaluation becomes more positive, while their evaluations of others become more negative. Power tends to weaken one's social attentiveness, which leads to difficulty in understanding other people's points of view. Powerful people also spend less time collecting and processing information about their subordinates and often perceive them in a stereotypical fashion. People with power tend to use more coercive tactics, increase the social distance between themselves and subordinates, believe that non-powerful individuals are untrustworthy, and devalue the work and ability of less powerful individuals.

So, think positive, and be a positive and powerful man. The public has the right to vote, and in a democracy, one vote is one value, so elect an honest and good candidate. Moreover, let's struggle and best efforts to become the Prime Minister, the Chief Minister, the President of India, General of the Army, the Governor, the Chief Justice, Justice, Judges, Member of Parliament (MP), Member of Legislature Assembly (MLA), MLC, MC, Election Commission, Human Rights Commission, SC/ST Commission, etc. and the Commissioner, Deputy Commissioner, etc. these people having authority and Political Power, can change the fate of the country and help to the public in large. So do not be crippled or socially crippled. Get the knowledge and be aware. Nobody will give you the Regime on the plate.

Earlier in 1400-1500 AD, Satguru Ravidass Ji preached about the power of education and organisation in their Holi Sloks, as written in the previous Chapter. Baba Sahib Dr B.R.Ambedkar Ji has taken the same line of action and has given an excellent Constitution intellectually to the country, which has given rights, equality, justice and freedom to all the citizens of India.

After that Shri Kanshi Ram Ji executed the process of capturing Political Power; as a result, Behan Mayawati Ji became the Chief Minister of Uttar Pradesh. Behan Mayawati Ji did hard work for the public welfare

Satsangat Mil Raheeai Madhaoo|
Jaise Madhup Makhira||
(Satguru Ravidass Ji) **Shabad || 16 ||**

Means; Regarding organisation as the honey bee with the bee hive; Common thoughts, Common Love, Common weapon (stink), Common Trust and respect and never fighting with each other.

123

By Capturing the Power:- Some examples of capturing power are "Violence or Harmony", Violence has not had a good result; even Satguru Ravidass Maharaj Ji did not teach or advise us about violence. However, there is no doubt that violence can change the scenario; for example, To fulfil the demand or capture the power and the same or similarities with the power in the Military Commander's command. For peaceful getting power, Design the network, make a web, like a circuit, create the environment, control the government agencies, and influence others to gain and maintain power. Power as evil or unjust as can be seen as an excellent Humanistic objective, so use positive power for the welfare of Society and service to humanity.

If the leader thinks about how to capture power?

Through Vote, agitation, peaceful protest, and Non-Violence way is the best and right way for the proper and last long time. For Capturing the Power, leaders **desire** to change the system and lead the masses. Raise the issues which are against the public and demand the rights. Realize the people that they (Shudras/Scheduled caste/Scheduled Tribes) are not independent and under slavery, even they can`t enter the Temple and have no land, natural sources like mines, minerals and other resources, i.e., Wealth, Health and Education institutions. All are in the hands of Upper Caste people (capitalists) etc.

So there are three ways to capture the power of the King. By way of **capture the political power, organize the religion and by becoming the ruler.** With the **Violence, Non-violence & Downfall** of itself by the ruler/King.

Dr. B.R. Ambedkar Ji has given liberty and freedom in the fundamental rights and this was a great achievement for our people, and that's why we are able to get the education and jobs etc. After that, Babu Jagjiwan Ram Ji helped the community. Shri Kansi Ram Ji organised our educated employees and became the founder of "BAMSEF", a big Organisation in India. After that, he formed a Social organization, i.e. DS4 (Dalit Sosit Samaj Sangarsh Samithi), to fight for their rights. When it became a force, he launched a Political Party, i.e. Bahujan Samaj Party. The party contested the election and, with hard work, captured the power of Uttar Pradesh without any violence. Non-violence policy made the way clear and Behan Mayawati Ji became the 1st Dalit Women Chief Minister in history and gave good Government without any discrimination.

"Those who share the same views are our friends."

"Jo Ham Sehri So Meet Hamara"

If one wants to change the system, one should know the philosophy of the Brahmanical system (Hinduism) and how they work against Shudra/Ashoot. A large community then can trace/find the solution by changing their concept or organising and fighting against all old and hateful discrimination done by the upper cast.

Since the Indus Valley civilization, the Aryans have ruled based on division and divided humanity into four classes (Varan Vibastha) and continued suppressing the fourth class (Shudras/Ashoot, i.e. Scheduled caste and Scheduled Tribes) and using the rule of Sham, Dham, Dand, and Bhed mean to use the method of all kinds of influences & manipulations to achieve the desired END. Its ENGLISH equivalent(s)/ is/are:-

(1) "ALL THE TRICKS OF THE TRADE."
(2) "BY HOOK OR BY CROOK."
(3) "BY USING WINE, DINE &/or FINE."

Hindu (Brahmanism) Granth Manu Smriti has also described this method to make a citizen crippled. That`s why Baba Saheb Dr B.R. Ambedkar has put it on fire. What is the meaning of this method?

Sam means: Concoction; use this for getting work done. If work has not done, then use.

Daam means: Giving money or Greed of wealth, gold etc. Till if work is not get done then, use the Bhed method

Dhand means: Punishment, torcher, Mentally and Physically.

Bhed means: Separate, divide. Use weak points and get work done. And the same method/caste system has been applied in India by the Brahmins (the upper caste society), forced the original inhabitants of India to become Slaves/labourers for a long time and still, it exists.

1. The Caste System in India does not represent a division of labour, but it is based on hate and birthright and has been falsely justified by moral and religious concepts. The Brahmins held most of the power in Hindu society, and they were priests, otherwise known as the spiritual and intellectual leaders of the society. "They devoted their time to studying, teaching, and performing their Job to making the system of supremacy as per the Vedas and Samriti for holding power by hook or crook.

2. The second Varna in the social hierarchy is the Kshatriyas, the rulers and warriors of the society. Their job was to "Protect, administer, and promote material welfare of upper castes within the society" (Nigosian 136).

3. The third in the social hierarchy are the Vaishyas, the farmers, merchants, and traders who really control the economy of India.

4. The fourth and last of the Varnas are known as the Sudras, who are labourers, the Chandalas or "untouchables" had a status so low below the poverty line and could not enjoy their rights even though they had no basic amenities.

So in the last, organize the people and capture the power & enjoy the freedom. Do not give your remote control in the other hands.

*****

Chapter - 17

Polity and Administration

Politics in India today is infested with corruption and nepotism. There is no denial of the fact that monarchy existed in Ancient India. But the most important point is that there was the decentralization of power. Welfare policy existed as a governing principle. The science of Public Administration was held regarding the concept of justice and human rights.

The department and the agencies of the Government which are most important to know the process and its way of working and powers in the democratic system as well as in the non-democratic Government, as like about the Ruler/King, President Secretariat, Prime Minister Office, Election Commission, and Supreme Courts/ High Courts and Subordinate Courts, National Investigation agencies, and UPSC, etc.

Agriculture, Textiles, Commerce & Industry, Defence, Finance, Health and Family Welfare, Home Affairs, Housing and Urban Affairs, Education system Panchayati Raj, Petroleum & amp; Natural Gas, Power, Railways, Road Transport & amp; Highways, Rural Development, Urban Development, Water, Resources, Women & amp; Child Development Youth Affairs and Sports Coal Personnel, Public Grievances & amp; Pensions, Law & amp; Justice, Parliamentary Affairs Science & amp; Technology, Culture, Steel, Labour & amp; Employment, Communications, Civil Aviation, New and Renewable Energy, Tourism Consumer Affairs, Food & amp; Public Distribution, Food Processing Industries, Chemicals and fertilizers, Mines, Shipping, Disinvestment, Tribal Affairs, Social Justice & amp; Empowerment, Micro, Small & amp; Medium Enterprises, Heavy Industries & amp; Public Enterprises, Statistics & amp; Programme Implementation, Development of North-East Region, Minority Affairs, Corporate Affairs, Earth Science, Drinking Water & amp; Sanitation, Department of Space. **All these are the Government`s agencies**.

Skill Development and departments which are unknown to many

persons. Therefore, there should be participation by the all community. Due to a lack of knowledge, can not be a good administrator.

At the time of the Maurya empire, and there after India, i.e. Bharat was called Golden Sparrow (Sone Ki Chiria), and Ashoka's empire stretched from Afghanistan in the west to Bangladesh in the east. It covered almost the whole Indian subcontinent except Kerala, Tamil Nadu, and modern-day Sri Lanka. Ashoka built many edicts all over India including in present-day Nepal and Pakistan. His capital was at Pataliputra (Patna) and had provincial capitals at Taxila and Ujjain. That`s why the original native of India has proud and after that, they lost their empire and became Shudras, untouchables and now scheduled caste/scheduled Tribes. The great civilization of the Indus Valley was famous for its great cities, advances in technology and their highly cultured urban centers.

The original native of this land were the Ruler of the Country. Now the time has changed and change is the law of nature. The efforts and struggle of the Shudras is unforgotten, how they face the challenges, become the slave and even then are thinking about, **how to become the ruler of the country.** That is why because of the Gurus, Saints, and leaders came and gave messages from time to time like Satguru Ravidass Ji preaches that:

Narpat Ek Singhasan Soiya Supne Bhaiya Bhikhari|

Achhat Raj Bishurat Dukh Paiya So Gat Bhayie Hamari||2||

Means: Just as a king happened to be a beggar in his dreams while sleeping and he suffered miseries as a beggar in his dreams despite being a king in reality; the same way, we are in a similar situation and we suffer endlessly being separated from the kingdom, we lost in the dream world.

There is a clear message: we should wake up to get rights and political power. Political Power is the master key to all solutions. So now the question arose about how we can become the ruler of the State/ country and what we should do to get the key to Power.

It has concluded that from the above examples and the history we can easily learn that nobody can win or fight for their rights without planning or understanding the system. The present Era is advanced Cyber technology, advanced information technology, and advanced thinking, so it is a time to educate the children and motivate them to act toward becoming the Ruler and get power for the benefit of humanity.

So, **learn about the leadership/Ruler, develop the leadership quality, organise the public and become the Emperor / Leaders, then march to fight and win the war.**

Satguru Ravidass ji gave us many examples and teaching that many other saints and leaders also show the path of victory.

We should not forget that **Manu** (writer of Manuscript) is still alive in a different shape, with few people who think themselves that they are Upper Castes, Capitalists, Fascists and Communal who believe in casteism, racism and against humanity. They all are barbarian in the modern world. If they are in power, it is not that they made us slave; we help them to enslave us. We, the working class, oppressed and so-called lower caste, run all their's departments that suppress us.

We should not take the Gun in our hands to fight them. We simply show our strength and raise our voices by refusing to obey their orders and against slavery or exploitation. That is organised non-cooperative and stopped their machinery working against us. We should tell the Rulers that they are not fair rulers. They made different schemes for different peoples yet called themselves civilized and upper caste/class. We should tell them that give us the same treatment and faculties as you give to your people, i.e. Social/economic equality and Justice, love and fraternity, as well as our constitutional right to education, health, medical and pension; we should not raise our hand before Ruler for begging our Rights, defeat them, push them out, from power, capture the power and become the Ruler yourself, as we have the strong majority in a democratic country. We should change the way, change the strategy, Change the old Concept, do not live in a dream. Even these corrupt and cruel rulers are making false promises and creating the illusion of keeping us away from power for a long period. We all struggle for our Rights, Equality and independence, living on the state s mercy as beggars but with different names only as they have given us.

So, to become a Ruler or part of a Government, one must be aware of the geography of the State, its culture, philosophy, social structure, economy, nature of the public and policies of the system. In addition, the departments and the portfolio management are essential for the Rule on the people, i.e. about the ministries of a country and how they work.

There are many stories and episodes in history about the civilization of humanity and religion as well as about the stories and planning to become the Kings and Rulers and how they have captured or became the Ruler or King of the state or country from the above discussion and information in the history we came to know about the strategy as well as the system and the policies of the rulers, how they had become the ruler of the country. There is much bloodshed in humanity but it is not the right path. Go ahead with the new strategy and a peaceful plan to fulfil your dreams in the actual world. Everyone should be skilled in the information system, how to receive and give the information, and properly receiving and broadcasting the message so that nobody can deceive you. One wrong message can create confusion/illusion in Society.

When you start the mission confidently, there will be no hurdle to stop you from fulfilling the concept of Begumpura of Satguru Ravidass Maharaj ji & very shortly it will become a reality.

There have been many revolutions throughout history, but here are some brief facts and reasons behind seven of the most significant revolts against rulers:

*****

Chapter - 18

The Revolutions

How revolution can be created or organized against the corrupt ruler can arise from various factors, including social, economic, and political grievances. Nevertheless, here are some general steps that can be taken to create or organize a revolution against a corrupt ruler:

- **Revolution** (1765-1783):- **The American colonists revolted** against British rule because they felt unfairly taxed and oppressed without representation in the British Parliament. They sought independence and created the United States of America.

- **French Revolution** (1789-1799):- The French people rebelled against the absolute monarchy and the privileged nobility who held most of the power and wealth. They sought greater equality, liberty, and democracy, ending the monarchy and establishing a republic.

- **Haitian Revolution** (1791-1804):- Enslaved Africans in Haiti rebelled against French colonial rule and the institution of slavery. They fought for their freedom and independence, establishing the first black-led republic in the world.

- **Russian Revolution** (1917):- The Russian people revolted against the autocratic rule of the Tsar and the oppressive conditions they faced. They sought greater democracy, land reform, and workers' rights, leading to the establishment of the Soviet Union.

- **Chinese Revolution** (1949):- People revolted against the corrupt, weak nationalist government and foreign imperialism. They sought to establish a socialist state led by the Communist Party, resulting in the establishment of the People's Republic of China.

- **Cuban Revolution** (1953-1959):- The Cuban people rebelled against the authoritarian government of Fulgencio Batista and the unequal distribution of wealth and resources. They sought to establish a socialist state, leading to the rise of Fidel Castro and the establishment of a communist government.

- **Iranian Revolution** (1979):- The Iranian people rebelled against the Shah's authoritarian rule and the perceived Western interference in Iranian affairs. They sought to establish an Islamic republic led by Ayatollah Khomeini, resulting in the overthrow of the monarchy and the establishment of the Islamic Republic of Iran.

These revolutions were all driven by a desire for greater freedom, equality, and justice and a rejection of oppressive and corrupt rulers. Whether the revolution/rebellion was successful and whether its goal was overthrowing the government, forcing policy change, or something else.

General Causes:- According to Aristotle, revolutions occur when the political order fails to correspond to the distribution of property, and hence tensions arise in the class structure, eventually leading to revolutions. Arguments over justice are at the heart of the revolution.

Rebellions occur when men are dishonoured rightly or wrongly and when they see others obtaining honours that they do not deserve.

If like-minded people join the movement when the government fails to redress their grievances. Revolutions occur when the other members display rudeness or disrespect. A revolutionary climate would be soon created, especially when the state officials become haughty, arrogant, and drunk with power or pay no attention to the genuine problems of the people.

This leads to a deep societal divide, especially between the state and the people. Over time, people's complaints against corrupt officials increase, culminating in revolutions.

Fear is a genuine and the worst enemy of man and human institutions. It disturbs the peace of mind and other emotions.

Revolutions can occur either out of fear of punishment for a wrong committed or a fear of an expected wrong to be inflicted on the person who is afraid.

Contempt is closely related to the revolution. This contempt can be towards rules, laws, political and economic situations, and social and economic order. The contempt is also due to inequalities, injustices, lack of certain privileges and the like.

Finally, revolutions are also the result of imbalances in the disproportionate increase in the state's power that creates a gap between the constitution and the society. In the end, the Constitution reflects social realities and the balance of social and economic forces.

If this balance is disturbed, the Constitution is shaken and will either get modified or perish. For instance, if the number of poor people increases, the polity may be destroyed. Similarly, having more numbers of rich in the government may lead to an oligarchical setup. Thus, any sharp differences in the polity would result in revolutions.

Regarding the political factors, issues such as election intrigues, carelessness, neglecting small changes, growth in reputation and power of some office, or even balance of parties lead to deadlock and foreign influence.

Some general steps that can be taken:

1. **Build a coalition:-** Form alliances with like-minded individuals and groups who share similar grievances and goals. This coalition can include activists, intellectuals, workers, peasants, students, and other social groups.

2. **Identify grievances:-** Identify the key issues that are causing dissatisfaction among the population, such as political oppression, economic inequality, corruption, or human rights violations.

3. **Develop a clear message:-** Develop a clear and concise message

133

that articulates the grievances and demands of the movement. The broader population should easily understand this message.

4. **Mobilize supporters:-** Use various tactics to mobilize supporters, such as public rallies, social media campaigns, or strikes. These tactics can help build momentum and increase the visibility of the movement.

5. **Plan actions:-** Develop a plan of action that includes specific objectives and strategies for achieving them. This plan should be flexible and adaptable to changing circumstances.

6. **Build international support:-** Seek support from international organizations, foreign governments, and other allies who can provide resources, legitimacy, and protection for the movement.

7. **Stay committed:-** Revolutions are often long and difficult, requiring persistence, determination, and sacrifice. It is essential to stay committed to the cause and to each other, even in the face of adversity.

It's important to note that revolutions can be risky and may have unintended consequences. Therefore, it's essential to consider the potential risks and benefits of revolution before taking action.

Remember, Peace is more important than War. While War may sometimes be necessary in certain situations to defend against aggression or protect human rights, it is a destructive and costly means of achieving these goals. War causes immeasurable suffering, including loss of life, physical and psychological trauma, displacement, and destruction of infrastructure and communities.

Suppose a person in a democracy is planning to become a dictator and planning to carry out a massacre with the help of the military and police. In that case, it seriously threatens democratic values and human rights. Here are some steps that can be taken to stop such a situation:

- **Raise awareness:**- Spread awareness about the situation through organization, social media, news outlets, and other means to inform the public about the threat to democracy and human rights.

- **Mobilize civil society:**- Organize civil society groups, human rights organizations, and other groups to condemn the ruler's/dictator's actions and call for an end to the plan for a massacre.

- **Seek international support:**- Engage with international organizations such as the United Nations, human rights groups, and other democratic nations to seek their support in putting pressure on the Ruler/Dictator to end the plan for a massacre.

- **Pressure elected representatives:**- Pressure elected representatives such as members of parliament or General Assembly to speak out against the plan and take action to stop it.

- **Use legal means:**- Utilize lawful means, such as filing court cases, or initiating impeachment proceedings against the authority/head of a government, to stop the plan for a massacre.

- **Nonviolent resistance:**- Consider nonviolent resistance methods such as peaceful protests, sit-ins, and civil disobedience to express opposition to the plan for a massacre and demand an end to it.

In contrast, peace creates a safe and stable environment where people can thrive and reach their full potential. Peace enables communities to build relationships and cooperation, resolve conflicts nonviolently, and promote sustainable development.

1. **Avoid confrontations:**- If you are in a situation where there is a possibility of conflict, try to avoid confrontations and seek ways to de-escalate the situation. Do not engage in physical or verbal altercations.

2. **Stay informed:-** Stay informed about the situation and any updates that may affect your safety. Follow the news and official channels for information.

3. **Stay prepared:-** It's important to be prepared for emergencies by having a plan in place and knowing where to go in case of evacuation or sheltering in place. Have an emergency kit with essential supplies such as food, water, and medication & defence.

4. **Practice self-care:-** Taking care of your physical and emotional health during difficult times is essential. Practice for self-care /self-defence by getting enough rest, eating healthy, and seeking support from loved ones or professionals if needed.

This involves investing in community infrastructure and services and developing skills and capacities to respond to emergencies.

If direct action is necessary to protect a community from external threats, it should be done in a way that minimizes harm and is proportionate to the threat. This may involve developing a defensive strategy that includes physical barriers, surveillance, and self-defense training, as well as developing relationships with local law enforcement or military forces. Then be a warrior.

It's important to note that in situations where barbarians or anti-humanity people threaten communities, balancing the need for protection with the rights and dignity of all people involved can be challenging. Therefore, it's important to seek guidance and support, and for defense, can we use self-defense weapons or how can we protect ourselves from massacre? Using self-defense weapons to protect a community or society from threats should only be considered a last resort, and it must be done following national and international laws. The use of force, including the use of self-defense weapons, must be proportionate to the level of threat faced and should not harm innocent individuals.

There are a few steps that can be taken to protect a community from such a threat:

- **Develop a safety plan:-** Develop a safety plan that includes evacuation routes, designated shelters, and emergency communication procedures. Make sure that all members of the community are aware of the plan and know what to do in case of an emergency.

- **Strengthen community bonds:-** Build relationships and cooperation within the community to promote a culture of solidarity and support. This can help to identify potential threats and respond effectively to emergencies.

- **Engage with authorities:-** Establish relationships with local law enforcement and other authorities to develop a coordinated response to emergencies.

- **Invest in community resilience:-** Invest in infrastructure and services that can support the community's needs and promote resilience in times of crisis. This may include access to food, water, medical care, and education.

It is a also duty of a leader to protect his peoples & reorganize them for future.

*****

Chapter - 19

India as Geographical / Political & its Population

Total Area of India with map:- India is the seventh-largest country in the world, with a total area of 3,287,263 square kilometers (1,269,219 sq mi). India measures 3,214 km (1,997 mi) from north to south and 2,933 km (1,822 mi) from east to west. It has a land frontier of 15,200 km (9,445 mi) and a coastline of 7,516.6 km (4,671 mi).

The current population of India is 1,418,681,623 as of Friday, May 12, 2023, based on Worldometer elaboration of the latest United Nations data.

Indian Structure of Society

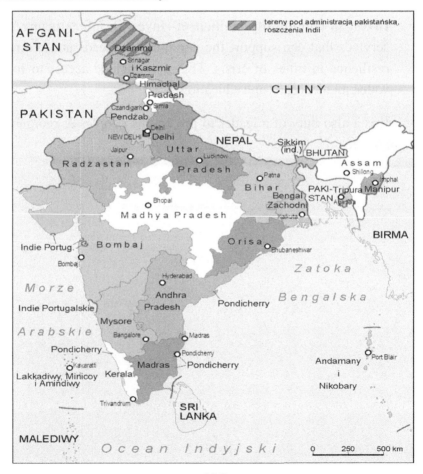

Chart of different religions with their percentage in India

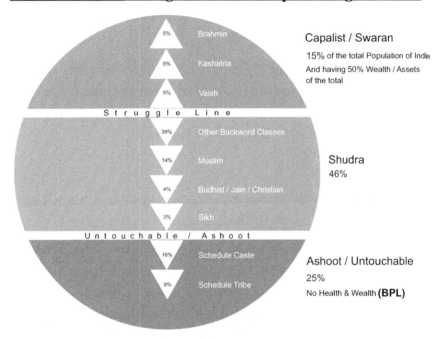

Main Sources of Public in India

Agriculture: 42.60% ·

Industry: 25.12% ·

Services: 32.28% · (2019)

The economy of India · List of megaprojects in India · Defence industry of India

It is ***the service sector*** which .. the main source of national income. Therefore service sector contributes more than 50% of the GDP. But it is the agricultural sector which employs more than 50% of the population. In that sense, more people in India are supported by agriculture.

The Capitalist/Vaishyas who are the business class have *90% of* the Indian wealth. They occupy most of the top bureaucratic and ministerial positions. They constitute the apex of the judiciary as well.

139

There are 229 million (22.9 Crores) Indians who still live in poverty, which is the largest number of poor people in a single country anywhere in the world. (04-Feb-2023)

From this Chart of different Communities/religions with their percentage in India, we can see how 12 to 15% of people are ruling and has captured maximum sources and 85% of people are discarded from their right. The reason is division in society.

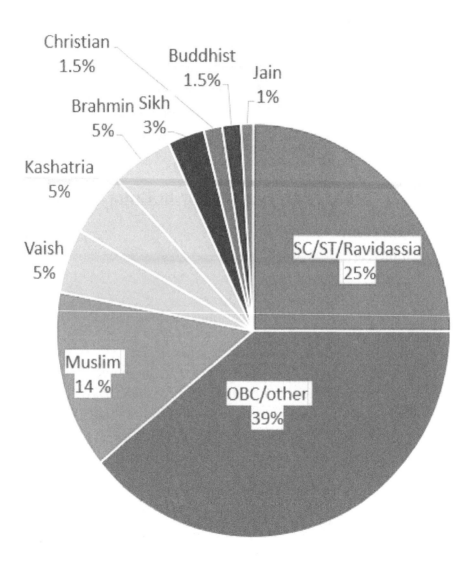

- The male literacy rate in the country is much higher at 84.7% as compared to female literacy rate of 70.3%

- The literacy rates in urban population is at 87.7% overall as compared to rural region at 73.5%. Even in urban areas, however, female literacy lagged behind male literacy rate

- India is ranked at 123 out of 135 countries in female literacy rate

- 50% of India's population is below the age of 25 and more than 40% are uneducated (2015 demographics)

- 10.1 million children working as bonded laborers

- 20 million children, between the ages of 3-6, that are not attending preschool

- Out of 100 students, 29 per cent of girls and boys drop out of school before completing the full cycle of elementary education

- 1 in 4 children of school-going age is out of school in our country- 99 million children in total have dropped out of school

- Out of every 100 children, only 32 children finish their school education age-appropriately **and these statistics are only going to escalate in the future, if not taken care of.**

India's job market suffers from a scarcity of good jobs, with hundreds of millions of people employed in informal, low-wage, insecure and precarious sectors such as agriculture. About 52% of workers are self-employed, having been forced to create their own jobs to earn an income. Lacs of children are going abroad to get the job and education.

Public Education Spending as a Percentage(Economies)

Statistical Publication. 2017

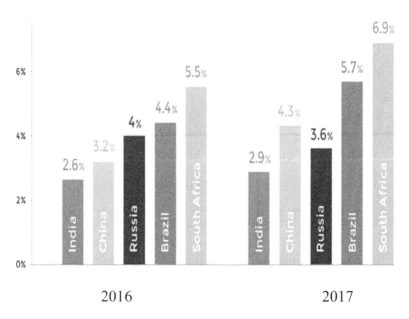

2016   2017

A Low Grade in Literacy In India:

Only 48 % of Females study up to the 5th grade

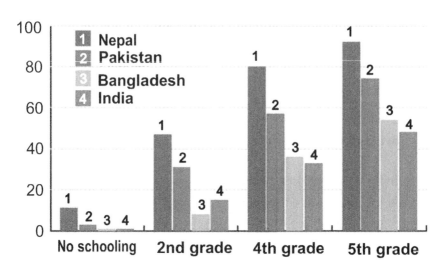

Source: Demography and Health Survey 2016 (OHS)

Child Labour in Numbers

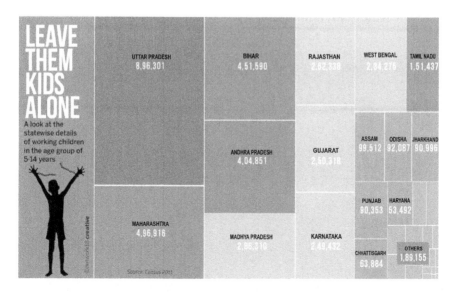

Constitution

The definition of the Constitution: The constitution is a political frame based on which principles or laws of a country are formulated. Under the constitution, the rights and duties of citizens are described. The relationship of people with governments is decided by the Constitution.

Suppose you became the Leader of the public and got the power and then became the Ruler and Ruler will have to develop a system in which way he works called authority/ Government and the Government will follow the Rule and regulations, legally written law, function, aims, and objects, which is called the constitution of the Country, for run the State? The Constitution should be written in detail, liberal, flexible as well as rigid, and accepted by the large community or public of the State/Country. Our Constitution of India is the best Constitution written with hard and noble work by the most educated and intellectual great personality Bawa Sahib Dr Bhim Rao Ambedkar (Bharat Ratan) the Symbol of Knowledge. It is no less than a religious book for the downtrodden.

Every state has their own Constitution in which the Rules, Regulations and principles or laws as per their traditions are followed and run by the Ruler/Government.

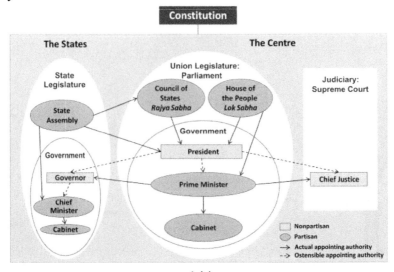

144

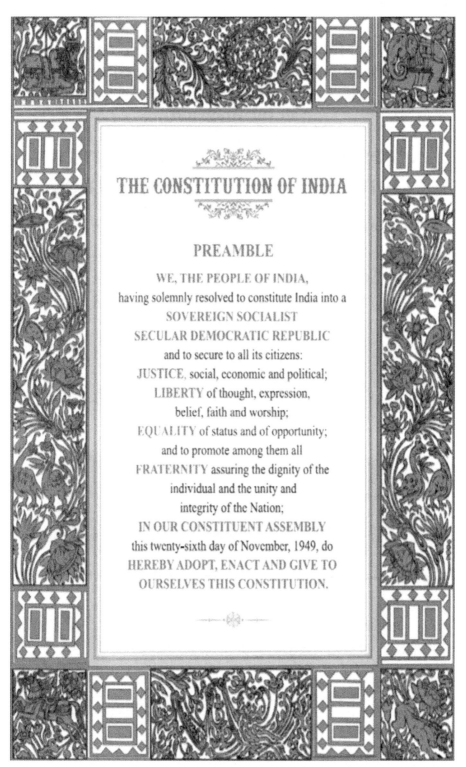

THE CONSTITUTION OF INDIA

PREAMBLE

WE, THE PEOPLE OF INDIA,
having solemnly resolved to constitute India into a
SOVEREIGN SOCIALIST
SECULAR DEMOCRATIC REPUBLIC
and to secure to all its citizens:
JUSTICE, social, economic and political;
LIBERTY of thought, expression,
belief, faith and worship;
EQUALITY of status and of opportunity;
and to promote among them all
FRATERNITY assuring the dignity of the
individual and the unity and
integrity of the Nation;
IN OUR CONSTITUENT ASSEMBLY
this twenty-sixth day of November, 1949, do
HEREBY ADOPT, ENACT AND GIVE TO
OURSELVES THIS CONSTITUTION.

A differents form of government in the democracy, the presidential democracy and parliamentry democracy as shown in the diagram

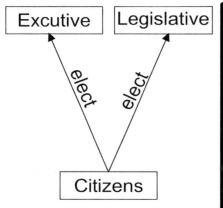

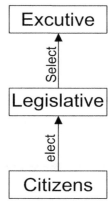

S. No	Presidential Form of Government	Parliamentary Form of Government
1.	President is directly elected by the People	Prime Minister is the leader of majority Party
2.	President is Supreme	Central Legislature is supreme

3.	Separation of Powers	Absence of Separation Powers
4.	Independent branches	Centralization Independent branches with Overlapping functions
5.	President - head of the State	President - head of the State
6.	President - head of the Government	Prime Minister - head of the Government
7.	Separation of Powers	Centralization
8.	Independent branches	Independent branches with Overlapping functions
9.	Individual Leadership	Collective leadership
10.	President is not accountable to Congress	Collective and Individual Responsibility

Chapter - 20

Formation of organizations and development of the religion:

The organisation and the development of religion mean the development of humanity, society, community, and the country. Therefore, there are some efforts to form organisations in the world and as well as in the country with the help of Organisations and cooperation with each other as mentioned below:

Dharam Guru	
Trust	
National Body	International Body
State Body	Country Wise
Distt. Body	State Wise
Village Body	District Body
World Wide Body	

Make the Digital Ravidassia **Directory** with full particulars i.e. **Name, age, Address , Occupation, Tele Phone and E-mail.**

NAME	AGE	ADDRESS	OCCUPATION	TELE PHONE	E-MAIL

148

List of Dignitaries, Lawyers and Solicitors, Professor Doctors, Journalist, PhD Schollers, Writers, Schools, Collage, Universities, Hospitals, Media, Social Media, Print Media, Film Industry, Actors, Directors, Singers, & How many Chief Minister, Ministers, Governors, Ambassadors, Hitachi, Mayor, Judges, in Supreme Court, High Courts & In the Distt. Courts, IAS, IFS, IPS, IRS, Officers, DC/ DM, Commissioners, SC/ST Commission, Military Officers (Defence Service)_Business Man /women Industrialist Builders Transporters_& List of Prominent Ravidassia in the World / India., Ravidassia Calendar

Business deals with the countries:- treaties, agreements: franchise, dealership. Agencies etc.**Providing** jobs and work permit

It is also a way to put pressure on the Government/Ruler to work and make policies for the welfare of the downtrodden. And should approach the Political Parties for projecting the Prime Minister / Chief Minister of state.

Create a pressure Group and declare the candidate for Prime Minister and Chief Minister of the Community; instead, the community will give Votes and support. The Prime Minister or Chief Minister candidates should be disciplined, As the population and proportion of Ravidassia are highest than others in India and are also living abroad,

Some Organisations are struggling for their rights and raising their voice against discrimination in different places and ways, but all are not doing it with cooperation. Now it is time, So now, join hands with each other.

The Main Organisation:-

1. Akhll Bhartiya Ravidassia Dharam Sangathan

2. BAMCEF

3. Bahujan Samaj Party (BSP)

4. Republican Party of India (RPI)

5. All India Dalit Mahila Adhikar Manch (AIDMAM)

6. National Campaign on Dalit Human Rights (NCDHR)

7.Dalit Indian Chamber of Commerce and Industry (DICCI)

8.All India Dalit Youth Association (AIDYA)

9.Ambedkarite Students Association (ASA)

10.All India Confederation of SC/ST Organisations (AICSO)

11.Bharatiya Dalit Panthers (BDP)

12.Bahujan Kranti Morcha (BKM)

13.National Dalit Movement for Justice (NDMJ)

14.Dalit Shoshan Mukti Manch (DSMM)

15.Dalit Solidarity Network UK (DSNUK

16.Azad Samaj Party

17.Dalit agricultural labour movement

18.Krantikari Pendu Mazdoor Union

19.Punjab Khet Mazdoor Union.

20.Zameen Prapti Sangharsh Committee

& many other organizations are struggling for their rights.

The latest Organisations have been successful in their task and ambition i.e.

Zameen Prapti Sangharsh Committee led Movement in Punjab-A turning point in Revolutionary history of Punjab and India

Upper-caste landlords forcibly seize land. Times children are made to go hungry. The sarpanches, with all their might, suppressed the democratic assertion of Dalits and sponsored attacks on them by goons of upper castes in the course of history the Dalit Community has been denied fundamental rights and marginalized, leaving no stone unturned. In 1961, the state passed the Punjab Village Common Lands (Regulation) Act, reserving 33% of agricultural village common land for Scheduled castes, who could get an annual lease through bidding. Rules under the statute were framed in 1964.

The Zameen Prapti Sangharsh Committee of Sangrur-Patiala, which has encompassed different areas. Positive that the lockdown did not dissipate the spirit of the Dalit landless labourers. Most methodically, they revived their democratic movement.

in Punjab. In the last month, a major resurgence has risen of the struggles of the Zameen Prapti Sangharsh Committee of Sangrur-Patiala, which has encompassed different areas. Positive that the lockdown did not dissipate the spirit of the Dalit landless labourers. Most methodically, they revived their democratic movement. A spate of protests erupted on the burning issues facing the Dalit community. Regions like Gharachon and Singla shimmered the spirit of resistance at its crescendo. Issues revolved around issue of distribution of panchayat land reserved, scrapping of loan re-payments and opposition to attacks of mafia elements on Dalit activists.

On June 8th one thousand Dalit villagers swarmed in Sangrur like an army and besieged the house of minister Vijay Singh Singla, demanding reserved panchayat land promised to them.

The president of the zonal committee of the ZPSC, "Our movement has so far been successful in 55 villages now, in Sangrur and Patiala district, where the Dalits get their share in the land through genuine auctions," Mukesh said. He said that there were 55 such villages, "each is a success story of the class struggle.

All organizations should catch hands of each other for achieve the goal.

*****

151

Conclusion

In last, a simple terms, the teachings of Satguru Ravidass Ji Maharaj provide us with valuable lessons on how to be good Emperor / Leaders and kind individuals. These teachings are timeless and full of wisdom. They guide us to be strong Emperor / Leaders who care for others and inspire them. One important lesson is to find peace within ourselves and with others. When we are calm and in control of our emotions, we can make wise and compassionate decisions as Emperor / Leaders. It's also essential to be disciplined and live a simple life, not just focusing on material things, but helping and uplifting others. Being honest and having strong morals are crucial traits of good Emperor / Leaders. We should be accepting and respectful of different beliefs and backgrounds, promoting a culture of understanding and unity. Seeking knowledge and using it wisely will help us face challenges and uncertainties effectively and for understanding the opponent's policies.

Religion, for "Begumpura" means having a deep connection with the divine and respecting all life. A real hero is not just brave physically but stands up for truth and justice. Emperor / Leaders should use their power responsibly and with empathy, inspiring others to be determined and pursue their goals. Resourcefulness is about finding creative solutions to problems, and generosity means being selfless and caring for others. Good leaders manage their responsibilities well, ensuring growth and prosperity for everyone they serve.

In summary, following the teachings of Satguru Ravidass Ji Maharaj will make us better Emperor / Leaders and citizens create a world where everyone can live happily together, free from suffering and inequality. By embodying these qualities and inspiring others, we can build a brighter and more compassionate future for all. Let's follow these teachings and become beacons of hope for others as we lead with wisdom and kindness without fear and avoiding all superstitious beliefs.

Sat Paul Virdi
BA LLB

Reference

www.derasachkhandballan.net

B. R. Ambedkar - online source

https://tamil.indianexpress.com › opinion

https://velivada.com > ... > India

online source › Simon Commission

https://www.sabrangindia.in›

https://www.britannica.com

online source › Poona Pact

https://www.hindustantimes.com>

Annihilation of Caste- online source

www.worldhistory.org

History of Buddhism in India - online source

online source, the free encyclopedia

Nanda dynasty - Britannica https://www.britannica com >

online source Maurya_Empire #Timeline

HINDU TEXTS THE VEDAS, UPANISHADS, BHAGAVAD
(https://factsanddetails.com>

Ramayana-World History Encyclopedia https://www.worldhistory.org

Pushyamitra Shunga - online source

 online source Shambuka

https://www.hinduismfacts.org hindu-caste-system

https//www.worldhistory.org The Ramayana

https://www.worldhistory.org image › gupta-dynasty-

online source › Mughal Empire

online source › Mahmud_of_ Ghazni

Babur - Founder of Mughal Empire, https://byjus.com>

online source › Maratha Empire

online source › Sikhs

online source › Mysorean_invasion

online source › Nizam of Hyderabad

online source › Nawabs of Bengal

https://prepp.in > news > e-492-the-bhakti-movement

https://www.sikhiwiki.org> index.php› Bhagat_Sadhna

online source › Namdev

online source › Bhagat Trilochan

online source. › Bhagat Sain

https://www.youtube.com> watch

Shri Guru Ravidass Ji Maharaj. https://www.pinterest.com › Explore Art

online source › Kabir

https://www.britannica.com › biography Guru-Nanak

Product sold by tallengestore.com

online source History of Sikhism

Facebook Sikh Models - All 10 gurus with their lives formed Sikhs:

https://in.pinterest.com/kamalkaur9/

m.timesofindia.com

Sikh Sikhi Sikhism

https://www.sikhsangat.com

online source › Ranjit Singh

online source › History of the British Raj

https://ohrh.law.ox.ac.uk> slavery-casteism-in-india-no..

https://www.gettyimages.in photos › slavery

online source › Caste system in India

Sabad Begumpura 3'

online source › Jyoti Rao Phule

https://bharatdiscovery.org> india

online source › Periyar

https://www.upgradingoneself.com › periyar-quotes

https://www.linkedin.com› pulse 7-ways-emancipate-y...

https://www.linkedin.com › pulse > baby-elephant-syndro...

https://www.goodreads.com > quotes > 9008454-the-mi..

https://www.goodreads.com > quotes 44867-believe-I.

https://www.goodreads.com> quotes > 519673-determi..

https://www.quora.com What-does-this-statement-mean-...

https://www.inc.com> marcel-schwantes warren-buffetts..

https://www.goodnewsnetwork.org> corrie-ten-boom-q...

https://www.goodreads.com quotes 10176719-none..

online source State (polity)

Essential Elements of State - Political Science
https://www.politicalscienceview.com

Kingdom Definition & Meaning-Memam-Webster
https://www.memam-webster.com.dictionary. kingd

The rise of Islamic empires and states https://www.khanacademy.org›

Online source › Spread of Christianity

https://online.champlain.edu blog student-stories-kj

https://google.com>serch

https://thelogicalindian.com › History

https://vachanbaddh.com>

Sabad-21, Jab ham Hote..., Amritbani

Online source › Manu_(Hinduism)

Printed in Great Britain
by Amazon